Th

Ten Pound Poms

Australia Bound

1964

John van Weenen OMT MBE

This book is a work of non-fiction. It is a true story that took
place fifty-four years ago and all characters, places and incidents
are as accurate as the author's memory permits. Dementia is not
an issue at this moment in time, but the author is abundantly
aware of its ability to descend indiscriminately on its next victim.
A clandestine liaison with a Mr G Reaper is in evidence for
together, they appear to have a total monopoly in servicing
mankind and are boastful of a never ending supply of human
fodder—or so they think. I'm on their case, they better take me
seriously—or else…

www.newgencration-publishing.com

New Generation Publishing

Books by the same Author:

The Beginner's Guide to Shotokan Karate

Advanced Shotokan Karate Kata

Shotokan Karate—the Definitive Guide

Karate for Children—Volume One—Basics

In Funakoshi's Footsteps

Task Force Albania—an Odyssey

Task Force Albania—The Kosovo Connection

Victims of Love

Dedication:

I would like to dedicate this book to the following people:

Lillian van Weenen
Leonard van Weenen
Derek van Weenen
Moss Hollis
Doris Duthie
Gavin Duthie
Eddie Whitcher
Paul Perry
Tony Robinson
Hilda Robinson
Geoff Dix
Mick Harton
Masutatsu Oyama
Joseph Maguire

All of whom are sadly no longer with us. R.I.P.

About the Author

John van Weenen's life has been 'eventful' to say the least. After a childhood of poverty in North London, he travelled the world and discovered Karate, eventually returning to Britain to achieve success by sheer hard work.

He developed his passion for karate, that most demanding of martial arts, first in Australia, after having arrived there with his two brothers as 'Ten Pound Poms' and then Japan, and later under the great Master Hirokazu Kanazawa, himself a student of the legendary Gichin Funakoshi (1868–1957). It was he who introduced karate to Japan from his native Okinawa in 1922. Funakoshi saw karate as more than a physical martial art form— for him it was the key to his philosophy of life; of responsibility to others: "Make benevolence your lifelong duty."

John modelled his own life on Funakoshi's precepts and followed in the Master's footsteps. He handed down the message of his mentors Kanazawa and Funakoshi to generations of new students to the art; encouraging his followers to help the needy.

Ultimately his teaching led to the giving of time and skills by many to a series of epic convoys of mercy during the nineties to help the starving and dying of Albania and Kosovo. He took British Doctors to Albania who successfully performed sight-saving operations on blind orphaned children. Finally, he commenced work on the British Children's Library Network, a scheme to bring basic education and computer skills to underprivileged street children.

He proudly accepted on behalf of all his students and helpers 'The Order of Mother Teresa' (OMT) and the MBE for services to the children of Albania.

John, with Mother Teresa in Calcutta in 1995

Contents

Prologue

Just who were the 'Ten Pound Poms'?

Allow me to provide a brief introduction to the Australian Government's Assisted Passage Migration Scheme which was created in 1945 and ran to 1972. It attracted over one million migrants from the British Isles, representing the last substantial scheme for preferential migration from Great Britain to Australia.

Assisted migrants were obliged to remain in Australia for two years after arrival, or alternatively refund the cost of their assisted passage. In 1964 when my brothers and I migrated, the cost of the ticket was £300. If they had returned within the two-year period, it would have cost each of them the £300 return fare plus the £290 paid by the Government to get them there in the first place. Now £300 sounds like a comparatively small sum but its equivalent today in 2018, taking into account inflation would be a staggering £5,595.00. Even the £10 the Poms paid, equates today to £192.50.

So it's easy to understand why many of the Brutish migrants, through no fault of their own, spent their two years in a Nissen Hut, saving hard, to raise enough money to buy return tickets to Britain. The cost of the return tickets for a family of four, two adults and two children, would have been equivalent in today's money to £16,785. It was obvious why the Australian Government provided little or no incentive to return to the UK. *The Poms had made their bed, so they should lie on it.*

There is no doubt The Australian Government's 'White Australia Policy' was racist, however, a quarter of all British migrants did choose to return to the UK, but half of these—the so called 'Boomerang Poms', returned back to Australia again.

Many people who have risen to prominence were 'Ten Pound Poms'. New Zealand's Julia Gillard was one. She migrated from

Barry, Glamorgan in 1966. Another Prime Minister, Tony Abbott, migrated in 1960. England's fast bowlers Harold Larwood and Frank Tyson took advantage of the scheme in 1950. The Jackmans migrated to Sydney in 1967 where son Hugh was born, and so on…

Looking back to the period after World War II, many Britons were sold the dream of a new life in Australia, seduced by the £10 fare. Government propaganda films in glorious Technicolor sold the dream of a modern British way of life *in the sun.*

It was a chance to escape post-war rationing and a housing shortage. Australia was sold as a land of enormous opportunity. In the first year alone, 400,000 Britons applied to emigrate, and Australia desperately needed white British stock to populate its shores and build its burgeoning post-war economy. The racist law known as the *'White Australia Policy'* meant blacks or Asians need not apply. Briton was more than happy to oblige, helping to populate the Commonwealth with Britons.

It's hard to imagine how things have changed in Britain and what a multi-cultural country it has become. Racism has had to be kept in check whilst Political Correctness has assumed greater status.

Over fifty years have gone by since I was a 'Ten Pound Pom'. So why should I have waited all this time to commit to paper countless memories of a bygone era that are as clear today in my mind as they were in those balmy days of the swinging-sixties. Some of the answers can be found in the following pages whilst others are less obvious and a touch more obscure.

What was never in doubt was my perpetual affinity to Australia and her people, regardless of colour or creed, who demonstrated their warm friendship. Our intention was always to go to Australia for the mandatory two years before returning. We were three young single boys, with no ties, looking for a way out of a mundane, suburban life. We all had a very basic education that left much to be desired, no skills, no prospects and no careers—we were going nowhere—and we knew it.

So when the advertisements appeared almost everywhere inviting Britons to come to Australia, often portrayed as *'a land of milk and honey'*, for the sum of £10, it was an offer just too good to miss. We saw it as a great adventure beginning with an amazing sea voyage and promises of employment, accommodation, sunshine and endless beaches. To *not* go would have been plain madness!

As I write these words in 2018, it seems a lifetime away from those first tentative steps my brothers and I took, as we boarded the SS *Iberia* at Tilbury Docks. Naturally we were a little apprehensive—who wouldn't be, but as we sailed from England to the other side of the Earth, fate decreed that I would meet a very beautiful girl and we would fall hopelessly in love with each other as we sailed into the unknown.

From the outset, this book was always going to be about the incredible time us brothers experienced during our two years in Australia—that was the story.

However, running in parallel to this and beginning by sheer chance on day one, is a love story of two people thrown together in times of uncertainty. Only in each other's arms did they find comfort, and for Joan, solace, following her father's death.

Combine both stories, as I've done here, and I hope the reader will agree with me, there is an intriguing read of a time gone by. A time when the Beatles, the Rolling Stones and the Hollies topped the charts, Perhaps it's just a coincidence and nothing more that on 21st July 1964, the day we sailed for Australia, twenty-seven-year-old John White, a footballer from Tottenham Hotspur was killed by lightning whilst playing golf—*at our father's club at Crews Hill.*

Things have changed a great deal in fifty-four years but the search for adventure continues unabated, as does the desire for true love in these precarious times in which we live.

I first read Robert Louis Stevenson's *Treasure Island* at ten years old and, like most other boys, I loved it. It wasn't until a year later, at a South Kensington Museum, that I began to learn about Stevenson the man.

Sadly, he died young, at the age of forty-four from a cerebral haemorrhage, but not before writing some incredible stories and it was *Treasure Island* and *Kidnapped* that really inspired me, and filled me with the urge to travel. Visiting Western Samoa and his tombstone high up on Mount Vaea with his words from 'Requiem' inscribed on it would be a dream for me, and is on my 'must do' list.

Requiem

Under the wide and starry sky
Dig the grave and let me lie:
Glad did I live and gladly die,
And I laid me down with a will.

This be the verse you grave for me:
Here he lies where he long'd to be;
Home is the sailor, home from the sea,
And the hunter home from the hill.

Robert Louis Stevenson
1850–1894

The Catalyst

In the latter part of 1963 I was consumed by wanderlust. I'd seen films, talked to a number of travellers who had been to other countries, and I wanted to go too. Comparatively few people seemed to travel abroad in those days. I remember being enchanted as a child by a film showing where Robert Louis Stevenson had been buried. I had a burning desire to go in search of adventure, not be stuck in working-class suburbia. I had no ties, nothing to lose, but much to gain.

Five friends were of like mind, and we met at 'The Plough' public house in Enfield to chat about the adventures we might have if we drove across Europe. I had an old Ford Zodiac car at the time which we were going to use. I attended to the administration and planning and obtained the relevant documents needed. In the six-weeks before we were due to depart, one chap dropped out, another couldn't leave his girlfriend, and another's parents wouldn't let him go, so we were down to three, then two. On the evening before our departure the following day, I had arranged to meet the last remaining member, and he didn't turn up. I remember the barman saying, "So, they've all left you have they?" and all I could reply was, "Yep," and I felt really let down. I thought, "Right! It's been a learning experience if nothing else. If you want to do something in this life, you've got to do it yourself and not rely on others." I'd had enough. It was 22nd November, and I'd had a bad day. I drove home and opted for an early night.

My mother woke me the following morning, with the shocking news: "President John F. Kennedy has been shot dead in Dallas." As news of his death reverberated around the planet, people worldwide were stunned, and just couldn't believe what their television sets and newspapers were telling them—and I thought *I'd* had a bad day! It put things into perspective, but did little to relieve the frustration I was experiencing after being let down.

In my mind I reflected back to my yearly holiday as a child. I was taken to the seaside annually by my father. He took me to Thorpe Bay, near Southend on his 'works' outing. I often wondered why I was the only child on the coach. They were all male affairs and the men would take crates of beer with them to drink on the journey. They would stop at a pub, usually the aptly named 'Halfway House' and they'd all get off, relieve themselves, have a drink, then get back on board for the final leg of the journey.

On arrival at the chosen watering hole in Thorpe Bay, quite inebriated by now, they quickly filed off and disappeared into the public bar where they stayed for the remainder of the visit. As children weren't allowed in pubs in those days, my father sat me on a wall outside the bar window. He came out to see me every hour with a lemonade and a large circular shortcake biscuit. I sat on that wall for hours, feeling quite alone and wondering where the sea was. I came to the conclusion perhaps the tide was out. Finally they would all appear and stagger onto the coach for the trip home. Strangely, they all insisted on making the halfway stop for a little more 'liquid refreshment'. That was my day at the seaside. It really wasn't much of a holiday for a seven year old boy—was it?

The Die Was Cast

On a bitter cold Monday in January 1964, I went to Australia House at the Aldwych, in London and applied to emigrate. I wanted to get as far away from Enfield and *friends* as I could; I wanted to start afresh on the other side of the world. My referees in Australia were descendants of Adelaide van Weenen, my great-aunt, who had married and taken the name Parslow. I knew about the Australian van Weenens through another great-aunt—Kate. I had three brothers in all—Garry, Jeff and Derek who was the youngest. Both Garry and Jeff wanted to come with me to Australia and I welcomed the idea but impressed on them, that if they changed their minds, it wasn't a problem, I was going anyway.

I thought it was going to be easy leaving home to go to Australia, but it wasn't. It was hard saying goodbye to my parents and my family, even though Jeff and Garry were coming with me. When we set sail on the SS *Iberia*, a twenty-nine-thousand ton liner of the P&O Steamship Company from Tilbury on Monday, 21st July 1964, I felt I might never see my parents again. Although we had been through good times and bad, somehow, when you say goodbye you only remember the good ones.

Sailing out of Tilbury was very exciting and as emotional as it gets. Thousands of 'Ten Pound Poms' lined the decks holding onto the rails, the streamers and the nylon stockings and all crying and waving to their families and friends far below on the key-side. Three loud and decisive blasts from the *Iberia* signalled our departure It was a poignant moment for all us passengers, as it was too for those assembled on the dockside.

Slowly, the gap between the huge ship and the dockside increased, inch by inch as the slack on the thousands of coloured streamers decreased. As they became ever more taunt, each friend or family member knew that any second the bond between them and their loved ones would be broken. Thousands of ahrrs could be heard as the tangled streamers fluttered to Earth.

All those gathered there that day, either on the ship or keyside, grew smaller to each other till all were lost in a sea of faces. Only one rope of nylon stockings, a hundred metres long, tethered the great ship—then it snapped too—freeing the *Iberia* as she sailed into the centre of the Thames, her bow pointing to the open sea and in the direction of the far-away Southern Cross.

What lay ahead over the horizon was unknown. It was exciting, daunting and just plain terrifying for most. Hiding your innermost feelings was so much more than 'difficult'. Perhaps those glossy colour photographs of Australia's beautiful beaches, paraded in abundance outside Australia House at the Aldwych, didn't tell the whole story! Whatever the truth, now there was no going back. In four weeks and 12,000 miles, all would be revealed.

Many would make a success of their new life down under, but a large number would not, and live every day waiting for their two-year sentence to run its course. Only then would their passports be returned to enable them to book their tickets home to Britain. Unfortunately for many, Great Britain was not the utopia they thought it was, and once back, *they realised their home was actually in Australia* and nowhere else. The tragedy was, they had to leave Australia for the reality to dawn on them, that sadly they had made a monumental mistake.

With the passing of time, many did return and finally became *'good Australians'*.

Young Elizabeth Taylor

In those days Australia was just about in every sense on the other side of the world, for we didn't have the technology we have today. Telephoning was often difficult with bad communication. It was a big step. The journey was going to take just over a month. My brothers and I were allocated our cabin on F deck, F529 to be precise, deep in the heart of the ship. In fact, you couldn't go much lower—the next deck down was Davy Jones' Locker! The cabin was six-berth, sharing with three other male strangers.

It turned out that a young lad called Johnny and his father Fred Greenwood from Blackpool, would occupy two of the remaining berths, and the last was taken by Tony Robinson, an electrician, in his late teens, who hailed from Manchester. It was an unreal atmosphere with six strangers (albeit three of them brothers) thrown together like that, with little in common other than the desire to seek pastures new. We got to know Fred and his son Johnny very well over the next few weeks, as we did Fred's wife Ruth and their daughter Susan.

At that time, they had no idea of the tragedy that would befall the family only four years after their arrival in Australia. Johnny had just passed his driving test and was out in his first car with three other friends when a front tyre burst and they drove at speed head long into a lamp post. Johnny was ejected through the windscreen head first and suffered catastrophic brain damage. His three friends received numerous injuries but all recovered with time. Fred and Ruth have given their lives to looking after Johnny who became totally paralysed and completely dependent on them. However, we knew nothing of this that July day in 1964.

After a short while there was a knock on the door, and an absolutely stunning girl, who looked to my eyes at least, to be Elizabeth Taylor's twin, came in, followed by an older woman. They turned out to be Tony's sister and mother—Joan and Hilda,

5

respectively. I tried not to look at Joan; but failed miserably. That evening, we all met for drinks before dinner. Fred's wife Ruth, was also there. The Fates had conveniently arranged that I should sit next to Joan; we got on well, and she told me her story.

Apparently, her father had suffered a fatal heart attack in March 1963 and the family had decided to start anew in Port Elliott, a coastal village south of Adelaide, where they had cousins, but it was all very much an unknown quantity and a really bold venture for them.

So began a wonderfully romantic month for sixteen-year-old Joan and me. By day we would swim and sunbathe, and in the evening we would all gather at one large table for dinner.

Looking back, it was surprising we got on so well, but at the time, I'm sure, we all needed one another. Each individual had their own reasons for making the journey, and all had *exchanged the substance for the shadow.* No doubt Fred and Ruth would never have undertaken the trip if they'd known of the misery to come in the years ahead. What they all thought of the three Enfield lads, I shudder to think.

With hindsight, I guess the voyage was part of the dream. Australia was the destination but the exotic places en-route that we would visit were an exciting prelude of things to come. For someone like me who had never been further than Thorpe Bay, it was simply Nirvana. I remember reading the sailing itinerary with such unbridled enthusiasm. As the ship left the Thames estuary and steered into the English channel and followed the coastline of northern France, we knew, at last we were on our way to the New World.

That night we were lulled to sleep by an almost imperceptible creaking sound and the gentle rocking motion of the ship.

Our cabin was on F deck and when I asked one of the foreign crew members later about G deck, he just looked at me incredulously and replied, "No G deck." It was then I realized we were on the lowest deck on the ship. We had no porthole because our cabin was below the waterline and would remain so for the rest of the voyage. We had no way of knowing what time it was, day or night, and when the cabin light was switched off at bedtime—it was black beyond belief!

The Bay of Biscay lived up to its reputation and the sea was rough. Many were sick and retired to their cabins after breakfast, clutching their bottles of quells. The next morning the *Iberia* steamed into Gibraltar and we had the day at leisure. Garry collected our packed lunches from the restaurant and we walked down the gangplank for the first time.

Gibraltar's Rock towered above all else and we picnicked close by, just out of reach of its famous apes. After the rough sea we had just experienced, it was good to be back on terra firma.

After lunch, we relaxed on the grass with some cold drinks and soaked up the summer sun. Hilda and Tony went into the town for a couple of hours and Garry and Jeff decided to visit the local fairground.

I drew Joan closer to me. She was wearing a faded red and blue dress, tight fitting, above the knee. Her long dark hair cascaded onto the grass around her shoulders and her blue eyes were

Happy in Gibraltar

closed. As I leant over and kissed her, she immediately responded

7

and threw her arms around my neck. It was nice to be alone together and we both wanted it.

At 8.00pm whilst having dinner we set sail for Naples. With a whole day to explore this fabulous city we were absolutely spoilt for choice. The Greenwoods joined us and the morning was spent at Sorrento, swimming and snorkelling and chasing the baby squid. Then it was off to Capri by ferry and a visit to the home of Gracie Fields, the forces sweetheart loved by so many. Pompeii would have to wait...

Back on board we were heading for Port Said at the eastern end of the Mediterranean Sea. The *Iberia* anchored off shore and was besieged by a flotilla of small boats all selling their wares. They would pass their goods on ropes to the passengers high up on deck. Amazingly—sales resulted.

The Ten Pound Poms
'Happy John', 'not so sure Jeff' and 'thoughtful Garry',
not a million miles away from 'bewilderment'.

Aden was an unmitigated disaster and the *Iberia* berthed only briefly. Passengers were advised not to go ashore and from the stories we heard from the small number who did, we were glad we followed the ship's advice and remained on board.

The next morning we were awoken by the gentle roll of the ship. She had left Aden in the middle of the night and was steaming on the long journey across the Indian Ocean to Bombay. It would take the best part of a week to reach there. Whatever surprises India had in store for us had to be an improvement on the last port of call.

Bombay

Arriving at Bombay was an enormous relief after a week at sea when the weather had been bad and almost half the passengers had suffered sea-sickness. The medical team had been totally overwhelmed. Sadly for me, I was not a good sailor and was terribly seasick, so much so that I couldn't stay in the cabin. Every time I went down to F deck I would immediately vomit. It was so severe I decided to spend all my time, day and night, on the top deck in the fresh air.

My brothers and Joan very kindly brought me light food from the restaurant but I had little appetite for anything. I just longed to be back on dry land and the six-hour stay in Bombay brought little respite.

Two days later we arrived in Ceylon and docked at Colombo. Being here for 48 hours allowed us to take a tour to different parts of the island. By general consent we chose to spend our time at Mount Lavinia and a full day on the beach. Our packed lunches were suitably enhanced with some delightful local wine and it was sheer bliss relaxing under the swaying palms.

Now it was on to Perth and the first glimpse of our new home. We would be a week at sea until we arrived and I prayed for calm waters.

By and large the weather was pretty good but we were heading into the Southern Hemisphere and winter. When the bad weather came, it did so with a vengeance.

Jeff van Weenen age 17 and on his way to 'down under'.
"Where exclaimed Jeff? I thought we were going to Australia."

10

A Stabilising Influence

Nearing Australia the weather turned foul and from my vantage point on the top deck it was plainly obvious we were heading into a violent storm. Reluctantly, I left my makeshift bed and headed down to the restaurant to join the others. I ordered some vegetable soup, dry bread and water—it was a gesture, nothing more.

Diners began departing as the ship rolled from side to side. Simultaneously, it started to pitch and toss—surely the crew would deploy the *Iberia*'s new stabilisers that we had all heard so much about. I looked at my soup bowl. Somehow it was managing to remain stationary, a lot more than could be said for its contents which appeared to have a life of its own. People were having trouble walking—a waiter fell over—it was very scary.

It was then that something quite frightening and unforgivable happened.

The following is pure supposition on my part and I can only speak as someone who experienced a mistake of monumental proportions. I was not alone, fourteen hundred other people did too. Whether it was a technical failure or human error to blame, we will never know. No answers from the tight lipped crew after the event were forthcoming.

As the ship rolled over to the right (starboard side) the port stabilisers were engaged and this had the effect of 'pushing' the ship further to starboard so it was almost lying on its side before it eventually righted itself. The port stabilisers seem to have been engaged again preventing a similar thing from happening on the left side. Although pure conjecture on my part and many others too, it would appear the port stabilisers were employed instead of those on the starboard side as the ship listed heavily to starboard.

The official report suggests a major breakdown and possible malfunction of the port stabilisers.

Maybe we'll never know the answer. I do however recall hearing one sarcastic passenger remarking, "Well what do you expect for ten quid?"

The above explanation concerning the stabilisers was pure supposition on my part but as I've now discovered, uncomfortably close to the truth.

If the *Iberia*'s catalogue of disasters had been known by the thousands of passengers who sailed on her, would many have changed ships?

As the reader will see from the page opposite, the *Iberia* suffered a catalogue of disasters during her eighteen years at sea before being sent to the breaker's yard. When the above incident with the ship's stabilisers occurred on our voyage in 1964, in bad weather, in the middle of the ocean, she almost rolled over—frightening isn't the word. Many of us for a moment thought the ship was going to turn completely upside down.

The SS *Iberia*'s
Appalling Catalogue of Disasters

This 29,000 tonne vessel was launched in January *1954* and after sea trials, undertook her maiden voyage later that year. She could carry 1400 passengers and a crew of 700. It was on that voyage she was grounded on the sandy bottom of the Suez Canal and listed to Port 15, degrees, where passengers in the First Class Dining Room were given a close-up first-class view of the canal waters.

On 27th March *1956*, offshore Sri Lanka, she collided with the tanker *Stanver Pretoria*. She received a sizable gash to her upper port deck and inflicted considerable damage to the tanker.

In *1961*, she had a major blackout near Auckland.

The following year, the *Iberia* was grounded again in the Suez Canal damaging her port screw.

Later in *1962* she lost a lifeboat in the Suez Canal, killing a sailor, and on leaving Auckland Harbour a month later, allowed salt-water to get into the cooling system, resulting in an electric generator breakdown.

In 1964, her port stabilisers broke down causing her to nearly roll over. (Our sailing.)

On 10th June *1966,* her turbine couplings failed off the coast of Kobe, Japan.

Later in *1967*, in Funchal, Madeira, she collided with the dock.

Again in *1968* in Funchal also, she suffered her second blackout.

Her first run in *1968* of the new Sydney to Southampton route didn't go well at all. *She caught fire*, had a third electrical breakdown, engine failure and suffered a fuel leak.

1969 saw a second stabiliser breakdown.

Finally in *1972*, P&O got the message and took her out of service.

And in *1973*, the *Iberia* was scrapped in Kaohsiung, Taiwan.

With lifeboats gone, the SS Iberia prepares to leave Southampton for the breaker's yard in Taiwan.

Finally after so many miles, Australia appeared on the horizon. The *Iberia* had made it and it was about to deliver its human cargo first to Western Australia, then South Australia, Victoria and finally New South Wales.

Freemantle, the gateway to Perth was all we had expected. Beautiful parks and beaches and a city of malls and safe pedestrian zones abounded. We took a boat ride along the Swan river (named after the famous black swans) and our very enthusiastic and informative guide showed us the palatial homes of the rich and famous that lined its banks. With hindsight, I personally would have preferred not to see all this wealth. Most of us had very little money at that time and found it hard to deal with being confronted with such wealth and opulence.

Then it was on to Adelaide, our destination, which, if you include the suburbs, was a city of just over half a million people at the time—a bit bigger than Perth. It's hard for many people to appreciate today just how great an adventure this was, for the vast majority of people in Britain then hadn't even been across the Channel to France.

Having fun in the sun but not the most sensible place to sit.

A Welcome to Adelaide

The final leg of our mammoth sea journey would be across the Great Australian Bight to the city of Adelaide two thousand miles away. This stretch of the Great Southern Ocean was known to be very rough on occasions but fortunately for us the weather forecast for the next few days was good.

After dinner each evening, Joan and I would walk along the deck and sit out for hours watching the sun set over the ocean, and then the emergence of a myriad stars in the heavens. It was beautiful.

The last day at sea before docking at Port Adelaide.

We dozed, intermittently, on a soft blanket spread out on the upper deck. The warm wind blew gently all night long; overhead the Milky Way glittered across the sky. It was bliss, and as we sailed on the last leg of our journey to the other side of the world, Joan and I fell in love.

While the three tiny tugboats manoeuvred the *Iberia* alongside her berth at Outer Harbour, Port Adelaide, Joan and I said our tearful goodbyes. Port Elliott was sixty miles south of Adelaide, and neither of us knew when we'd see each other again. Although I had very little money, I assured her that as soon as I secured a job I would come and find her. There were thousands of people on the dockside. I scanned the crowd in the hope of seeing her once more—but she was gone.

Prior to disembarkation, we were split up and directed to different gangplanks. This was not done by gender but in order to keep families together. The final destination was also taken into consideration.

As we three boys walked down our appointed gangplank, our relative and sponsor, Doris Duthie, the grand-daughter of Adelaide van Weenen, began waving to us from the quay. She was accompanied by her son Gavin, his wife Narean and Gavin's younger brother Michael. They were a lovely family and made us so welcome and Doris had laid on a special meal for us at her house in the suburb of Wayville.

A Message from Col. William Light

I thought Adelaide was a delightful city, perfectly planned by the architect, Col. William Light, and regarded at the time as Australia's City of Culture. Light had designed the city, with its squares and wide streets, so that beautiful parklands—the first 'green belt'—surrounded it. His twenty-feet-high statue was erected in a commanding position, flanked by eucalyptus trees, with outstretched arm pointing across the River Torrens to North Terrace and the city beyond. A plaque bearing an extract from his log, the words of which I learned by heart, read as follows:

"The reasons that led me to place Adelaide where it is, I do not expect them to be generally understood at present. Mine enemies however, by disputing my validity, have done me the good service of placing the whole of the responsibility upon me. I am perfectly willing to bear it, and I leave it to posterity, and not to them, to decide whether I am entitled to praise or to blame."

Colonel William Light (1786–1839)

Adelaide was built on a grid system like New York, so finding one's way around was a straightforward matter. The river Torrens flows through the heart of Adelaide and meanders lazily through the picturesque parklands. However, all cities have their darker side.

Doris had done her best for us and booked us in at the YMCA for a few days, but it was a truly awful place. The accommodation was dirty and cheap; and bearing in mind we'd arrived in winter—cold. There were some very odd people there, down-and-outs, junkies, and the like. My brothers and I felt very homesick at that point—we were ten thousand miles away after all, from everything we'd ever known—and now we found ourselves in this dreadful place. It wasn't Doris's fault, she had no idea whatsoever what it was like and in fairness to her, she had gone through the complex procedure of sponsorship.

We decided to get out. Jeff and Garry had practically no money. I had left my savings in a Post Office account in Enfield in case of an emergency. With interest, it had accumulated to one hundred and sixty-five pounds, which I had transferred to the Commonwealth Bank in Rundle Street. It eventually arrived after two very anxious weeks of waiting. Gavin had very kindly lent me a little money to tide us over till it came, when I immediately paid him back.

We went to a recommended estate agent and found a property at Adelaide's Henley Beach. The first month's rent for the house amounted to twenty-six pounds and we paid it up front.

Strangely, one entered the building through the back door, from the main Military road, and the front door which was seldom used, opened directly onto the sandy beach. It was lovely, and seemingly a million miles from Canonbury Road, Enfield. Just to get out of bed in the morning and walk barefooted out through the front door onto the sand was a wonderful feeling.

The warm shallow water just beckoned you to come in…

Who Said,

"Blood's Thicker Than Water?"

My great-aunt Kate had asked me to look-up our great uncle, Rudi van Weenen, a very successful builder who lived near Port Adelaide. I decided to go alone, thinking it might be better at first rather than the three of us turning up on his doorstep. I had his address safely in my wallet and left the city late afternoon. I felt very excited about meeting another van Weenen, yet just a trifle apprehensive. After taking two buses and walking for miles, I finally arrived at his house early one evening, tired out. I knocked at the door and a man about sixty-five to seventy years of age answered it.

"Mr van Weenen?" I enquired.

"Yes," he replied.

"I hope I'm not disturbing you but I'm afraid I didn't have your telephone number, otherwise I would have rung. My name's John van Weenen; I arrived here from England two weeks ago and I was so looking forward to meeting you and saying hello." I held out my hand…

Now, most houses in Australia have a fly screen on the outside of the front door, as his did and he didn't even open it, he just looked at me through the tiny strands of wire and made no attempt to shake hands with me at all.

"And how are you?" I asked.

"I'm fine and you?" came his response.

Through the screen I explained that my brothers and I had emigrated to Australia and were going to live in Adelaide, and that great-aunt Kate in London had asked that we visit him and say hello.

"Well," he groaned, "you've said it haven't you?"

"Yes, I have," I said, somewhat shocked by his brevity and hostile attitude.

"Good day," he replied, and without further ado, disappeared inside and shut the door.

He just didn't want to know me. I felt like swearing but was too hurt to do so. To think, he was the only surviving van Weenen in Australia, and I'd come all this way to see him, and he hadn't the decency to ask me in, let alone offer me a cup of tea.

I found myself staring at a blank door and I felt almost paralysed. Tears were running down my cheeks—I quickly wiped them away using both hands just in case he'd had a change of heart and should open the door and see me crying.

Wishful thinking I thought to myself—he's gone…

Turning around, I retraced my footsteps down the path, shut the gate and walked away. My stomach was in a knot, I was crying again, but inside this time.

I never looked back and I never saw Rudi van Weenen again.

In the words of Noel Coward, it really was, "A Brief Encounter."

The Six o'clock Swill

Adelaide was considered a cultural city, quiet, sleepy and years behind the times. In the sixties, the Australian Government had a policy of increasing the population by encouraging European migrants to settle in Australia. The British were pretty much accepted as many Australians could trace their roots back to Great Britain. When the Italians arrived in considerable numbers, the average Aussie wasn't so keen on the idea. Within a short period of time the Greek invasion got under way and for some unknown reason, they became the bad guys. Fortunately for the Italians, this took the pressure off them and our average Aussie found them quite 'acceptable'.

The city's nightlife area in Hindmarsh Street was miniscule in 1964, however, the Italians and then the Greeks were doing something about that. The Poms (British) didn't get a look in.

At that time, the pubs in Victoria and New South Wales closed at ten o'clock in the evening, four hours later than their counterparts in South Australia where offices and factories closed at five or five thirty. This resulted in a massive problem, especially in the summer when temperatures were high and throats were dry. Workers had only a short time to get to the pub for a beer. Alcohol was not available for purchase after six o'clock and in Adelaide and the remainder of South Australia, this became known as 'the six o'clock swill'.

To get round the law governing opening and closing times, people would go into a bar just before six o'clock and order ten pints, or ten schooners, or ten midis and line them up in a straight line and proceed to drink them one at a time. The law governing the time they were allowed to finish drinking was thirty minutes. I remember seeing lines and lines of beers on the bar at six o'clock and all had to be consumed by six-thirty—or lose them. Every person knew which was his or her line—taking from the wrong line meant trouble, big trouble and this usually materialised anyway when the six-thirty deadline arrived. Consuming ten pints of beer in thirty minutes would be no mean feat for us ordinary mortals but to 'Aussies', it was a mere 'walk in the park'. *How they loved their 'grog'.* When it came to beer, they were quite indefatigable.

With time and a change in the law, South Australia fell into line with all other states and the 'six o'clock swill' became a thing of the past.

They just drank more—over a longer period.

Freedom and Horseshoe Bay

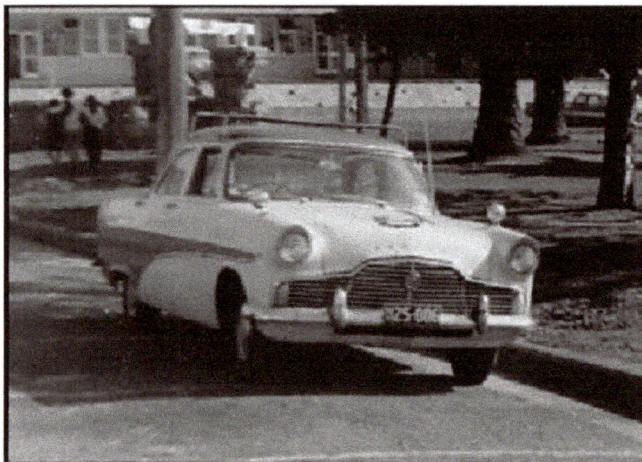

With the exception of the first month's rent, the balance of my savings went on a deposit towards a car. I was desperate to see Joan, and without hesitation I acquired a blue and white Ford Zodiac. My brothers and I walked into Ern Bateup's car showrooms in Hindmarsh Street, did a deal, collected the car and with a map at the ready set off for Port Elliott. The Robinsons were living in a caravan on a site at Horseshoe Bay, some sixty miles south of Adelaide. Parking the car, I asked where Joan was, and hurried across the sand dunes to find her. There, sitting all alone, quite forlorn, by the water's edge, was my sweetheart. I was told later that she'd come here every day and just sat by herself for hours at a time.

The Great Southern Ocean stretched out before me. I called out to her, but she couldn't hear me due to the almost deafening sound of the waves breaking on the beach. Suddenly she turned, saw me and we both ran into each other's arms. It was a wonderful moment, and one that I will never forget. For the next two years we spent little time apart, other than my trip to the east coast. She became one of the family, and Garry and Jeff became very fond of her.

My reunion with Joan at Port Elliott was incredibly moving. We had missed each other so much during the weeks we had been apart and it was heaven just to hold her once again. She hadn't got over her dad having that fatal heart attack in their Manchester home and her widowed mother, Hilda, was very brave in deciding to start a new life in Australia with her two children. After leaving bustling Manchester, all their friends and familiar surroundings, they felt totally isolated living in a caravan park on the other side of the world.

I know Joan really missed me as I did her. Her brother Tony, two years older was floundering somewhat, he needed to establish himself, make his mark which in the fullness of time he would do. He felt a little lost and as a man, rather inadequate whilst Hilda was still grieving deep down for her husband. It was all still fresh in her mind, but she was handling it well and I respected her enormously. Sometimes, when we were all together, I would glance across and see a tear in her eyes, and I would know she was somewhere else in her thoughts.

Early Days

The family decided to apply for a house north of Adelaide in the town of Elizabeth, a designated area under the auspices of the Australian Government which was largely populated by British migrants. Hilda's cousins understood the situation and were extremely supportive and six weeks later helped them to move. From that moment on, things improved. Hilda made friends with other British folk and started a part-time job. Tony and Joan also found work and my brothers and I were only forty minutes away by car.

Being staunch Roman Catholics, the local church welcomed them with open arms and this further helped them to integrate into local society. Each Sunday, Joan and I would drive north and visit different churches for Evensong. We were always made most welcome by the ministers and their congregations which often could be counted on two hands, as the outlying villages were so small but so welcoming. The services were not so much religious but social, when the community would come together and after the service would have a barbecue and the compulsory 'liquid refreshment'.

Joan explained to me early on in our relationship she would not make love to me until we were married and I respected her wishes—and we didn't. I loved her so much that I never let it become an issue. At times when emotions were running high, it was somewhat difficult.

For her seventeenth birthday I took her to a beautiful restaurant for dinner, high up in the Mount Lofty Ranges. From our table the sight before us was amazing with a panoramic view of the city of Adelaide far below. For me it was a moment to remember and sometimes I wonder if it was for her too.

With Hilda and Tony settled in Elizabeth in the new family home, Joan and I decided to take a short holiday together and explore South Australia. Going north would take us to Port Pirie and Port Augusta whilst heading south seemed the obvious choice and the beautiful Great Ocean Road to Victoria. "You choose, Cookie," she said. I leant over and kissed her.

Hilda was fine about it and she knew without a doubt I would look after her daughter. Joan's school where she worked as an administration secretary was closed for half term, so it was an ideal time for her to get away.

I'd learnt much more about her in recent weeks and I was slowly building up a picture of her life in the Manchester suburb of Levensulme. By coincidence, or maybe not, her dad had been a secondary school teacher for twenty years and had it not been for his failing health, would have been made head teacher at Every Street in Ancoats, Manchester where he worked with many deprived children. His tragic death from a heart attack took place one Sunday morning, just prior to the family leaving for Mass.

Tony took it the best but was naturally very upset, whilst Joan and her mum were devastated. After the funeral, Tony went back to his work as an apprentice electrician but Joan stayed with her mum for two weeks until she had recovered sufficiently. Becoming a widow at forty-eight was not what Hilda had ever envisaged in her worst nightmares and it decimated the family beyond belief.

Joan was only fifteen when she lost her dad but returned to college soon after to resume her shorthand course at Pitman's close by. She was always popular with her classmates but understandably became a somewhat introverted girl after her dad's death. Fortunately things improved gradually with time.

Tony Robinson, Susan Greenwood, Hilda Robinson, Joan Robinson

It was Joan who eventually suggested the idea of emigrating to her mum and brother, which initially received a lack-lustre response from both. It wasn't until one autumn evening when all three sat watching a film on television. The movie was Neville Shute's *A Town Like Alice*, and it made quite an impression on them all.

This photograph shows the SS Iberia at the
International Passenger Terminal, Circular Quay,
ten days after we had disembarked at Adelaide in 1964.

Perhaps it was time to think about a new life and one week later, Hilda wrote to her cousins in Adelaide to explore the idea of migration and the possibility of sponsorship. After all, she had spent some childhood years in Australia before returning, as her mother couldn't stand the heat. In the three weeks it took before a reply dropped through their letterbox, the notion of upending and starting a new life in Australia became more exciting with every passing day.

By the time, and it would take best part of a year to complete all the formalities, Joan would have finished her college course and

Tony would be a fully-fledged electrician, and both would be assured of securing good positions in the workplace.

Hilda opened the airmail letter very gingerly—it was good news! The cousins would be delighted to sponsor Hilda and her children and looked forward to hearing exactly what was required of them.

The first step was to visit the Australian office in central Manchester, which they did. After much form filling, document exchanges, and medicals, the Robinsons finally left their life behind and arrived at Tilbury docks on 21st July 1964 to board the ocean liner that would take them across the world to South Australia. They were excited, positive, yet full of understandable apprehension as they sailed into the unknown.

Our First Holiday

Although I didn't have an exact idea of where Joan and I would be going on our first holiday, I was able to give Hilda a rough guide and we promised to ring her every few days. The night before we left, we poured over the map. Garry and Jeff were excited for us and wished us a great time.

Driving south from the city we soon passed the beaches of Noarlunga, Seaford and Moana before the forty-mile drive to Victor Harbour where we intended staying for the night in a B&B. It took all afternoon to do it but there was no rush. We were together, in love and happy beyond compare, consumed totally by an overwhelming sense of freedom.

By luck, I found a perfect B&B, close to the harbour, which was inexpensive and quaint. We slept together as we had done a lot but I was always careful not to cross that single red line that remained so important to Joan. After breakfast we set off on the coast road heading south that would eventually take us into Victoria—it was a long way off but we had all the time in the world.

I knew the Zodiac would get us there and back, and it had been serviced a week earlier. Ten miles away was Port Elliott and we arrived there in thirty minutes. Joan leant over and kissed me. "I don't really want to go there—it brings back too many memories, would you mind if we didn't stop there," she said. "Of course not," I replied. Let's go straight to Goolwa where we can take the car ferry to Hindmarsh Island.

Crossing the estuary by ferry was an adventure in itself. It was a prehistoric affair that involved two ferries, moving simultaneously and both crossing from opposing banks. Somehow and I'm yet to understand how, both were controlled by underwater chains. It was as if one pulled the other, for both departed and arrived at the same time.

As we reached the opposite bank, the ferry-man raised the front rail and gave me the go-ahead. I carefully drove the Zodiac onto Hindmarsh Island and so on eventually to the town of Meningie.

The Coorong beckoned

The Coorong and 'Storm Boy'

I had recently read a book called *Storm Boy* which I had not talked to Joan about for I wanted to surprise her by bringing her here to the Coorong where Colin Thiele's novel took place. It was the story of a reclusive father 'Hide Away Tom', his son Mike and an Aboriginal man named 'Fingerbone Bill'. In it the boy befriends a pelican here on this ninety-mile stretch of virtually uninhabited beach.

Storm Boy and his father lived alone in a makeshift shack amongst the sandhills between the Southern Ocean and the Coorong—a lonely, narrow waterway that runs parallel to a long stretch of the South Australian coast. Amongst the teeming bird life of the Coorong, Storm Boy finds an injured young pelican whose life he saves. From then on, Storm Boy and Mr Percival the pelican become inseparable friends and spend their days exploring the wave-beaten shore and the drifting sandhills.

Mr Percival learns to help Storm Boy's father and warns the other birdlife whenever poachers are coming, but his part in rescuing a shipwrecked crew leads to great changes in Storm Boy's life.

Little did I know, that in years to come, Thiele's book would be made into an amazing film that would mark the beginning of the Australian Film Commission's entry into the International World of Cinematography where it won many awards. That was in 1976 and forty years after that it was remade *again* and proved to be another huge success. When asked what its appeal was, the film's director said it was about the relationship between a child and an animal, and in this case, Mr Percival a pelican.

Between us and the next watering holes of Policeman's Point and Chinaman's Well are ninety miles of very little. From the coast road we could hear the huge waves thundering ashore from the Great Southern Ocean.

Joan looked at me, "Come on, Cookie," she said, "let's go and explore this beautiful beach that you told me is totally deserted." Over the past two days she had affectionately begun to call me Cookie and I asked her why? She laughed out loud, "You really don't know do you?" "No," I said. Smiling, she put her arms around my neck, kissed me briefly and said, "Because you John-boy are my Captain Cook! I love your spirit of adventure and it must be contagious for I'm beginning to feel the same way as you." Well, what could I say. We just had to go. Collecting two bottles of water, sunglasses, hats and sun lotion, we parked the car and set off to find this incredible beach.

"How far do you think the ocean is, Cookie?" Joan asked.

"I don't know darling, but I have a feeling we're going to find out."

We began walking.

Young Love on a Deserted Beach

I tried to estimate it. "It's hard to judge, could be a couple of miles." For the next half-an-hour we walked across the sand dunes, listening to the waves and thinking we must be nearly there by now. It was so deceiving. "We have to keep going John, we can't turn back after all this," Joan said. Another thirty minutes later we were still not there and I reckoned we must have walked three or four-miles but the sound of the waves was getting louder. The sun had climbed higher in the sky, it was getting hotter and we were both feeling it.

"Come on Joan," I said, "let's go to those big sand dunes way up ahead and look beyond and if the sea is not there—we'll turn back." In what seemed like an eternity, two tired and frustrated people struggled to the top of the huge dune—"Eureka! The bloody Coorong," I shouted.

Joan was about to tell me off for swearing but was stopped by the absolute splendour of the sight that greeted our eyes. The sea was only a hundred yards away. I'd told her the story of Storm Boy while we were walking—now she could appreciate it. We sat down on the soft yellow sand and stared at the waves—they were magnificent and took our breath away.

We drank some water and just sat there mesmerised for a while. Then I spread the towels out and as we stretched our aching limbs, I pulled her close and kissed her and started to undo her blouse.

She immediately asked me what I was doing—"people might see," she said.

"What people Joan? There's no one here at all, we're alone." She raised her head and peered left and right along the beach. "You're right Cookie we are alone—absolutely alone."

She sat up for a moment, slipped her blouse off and laid back. She was wearing only a pair of shorts and pulling me towards her, kissed me passionately on the mouth. It was obvious to us both we were approaching the red line, but there was still some distance to go. "Take this off," she said, as she tugged at my shirt sleeves. "It's so hot and so incredibly beautiful here."

My senses reeled. I could feel the hot sun on my skin—smell the salty spray in the light wind from the ocean, as I held her slender girlish body in my arms. She in turn was aware of my hands caressing her which seemed to arouse her in a way I'd not seen before. She kissed me again and again in an attempt to get more satisfaction out of each kiss, then laid her head on my chest and I held her close. The moment overcame us both simultaneously. We looked at each other, full of love and wonderment—we were one.

A dozen 'Mr Percivals'

I wanted to take a dip in the sea but it was far too dangerous, so we paddled, hand-in-hand in the cold water. It was 4.00pm and we knew we had to say goodbye to our Shangri-La. "I want to come back here when we are married," she said. "We'll do that darling," I replied.

With that, we packed everything up and began retracing our footsteps back to the car and an hour-and-a-half later we made it. I started the engine, Joan took out the map and we pointed the Zodiac's bonnet in the direction of Chinaman's Well and hopefully, relative civilisation.

It was a simple matter of following the coast road and the absence of turn-offs for seventy-five miles made Joan's navigational skills redundant. The dirt road was fine. We had good tyres on the car and a full tank of petrol and were both in good humour as we set off.

She began laughing. "What is it?" I said. "Do you think they'll have a Chinese restaurant there?" Asked Joan. I looked at her and laughed myself. "Well! They should have but I wouldn't put any money on it darling." My taste buds were being aroused—"I wouldn't mind some crispy duck." "Me too," she replied.

The blue and white machine had performed well and within a couple of hours had brought us safely to Chinaman's Well. Naively perhaps, we were expecting a small country town but all that stared back at us was a small caravan park consisting of twenty vans and a communal toilet. That was it. Even the well had dried up many years ago and as we were about to find out, there wasn't a Chinaman in sight.

The Bats of Naracoorte

It was now eight o'clock in the evening and almost dark and with the nearest town fifty-miles away, the sensible thing would be to stay here. The lady in charge of the caravan site was lovely. "You two young things can have this little beauty," she said. "And it'll only cost you three dollars for the night. It's got water and bottled gas for heat and light and you'll sleep like babies." In the small 'Deli' that she also ran, we were able to buy some almost frozen bread, that would quickly thaw out, two tins of baked beans and a packet of salt and pepper. Doris, as we came to know her insisted we take two of her special cold beers to wash it all down with.

I heated the beans on the little gas stove and 'grilled' the bread. In the meantime, Joan had set the table—knives, forks, two glasses and our little packet of salt and pepper. So at nine o'clock that evening we dined like royalty on beans-on-toast and drank each other's health with genuine Aussie beer and boy—did it taste good. Three hours after that ludicrous six o'clock shutdown, we were drinking unfettered, in our first home—something we would remember forever. We fell asleep in each other's arms watching a myriad stars twinkling through the bedroom window.

The next morning we left the Coorong behind and headed towards Kingston SE and then on to Naracoorte, a town famous for its Bat caves. The small hotel we stayed at suggested we take a tour of the Bat caves which is taken in two parts. The manager very kindly booked the tour and we were picked up by coach mid-evening, just before twilight, and taken directly to the Bat caves. Once there, we all waited patiently and quietly for the Bats' nightly migration. As we waited I squeezed Joan's hand in anticipation. First a handful of Bats took off from the caves walls and ledges, then in a flurry of excitement, flapping and noise, literally thousands upon thousands left their home for the night.

The darkening sky blackened in an unforgettable exodus—and they were gone. Only us human spectators would precede their return at about five o'clock in the morning just before the first rays of the sun heralded a new day.

That night we went to sleep, full of anticipation again, partly for the 4.00am alarm call, but mostly for witnessing the obligatory return of a million bats to their home. Like everyone else that morning, we were in awe as the Bats returned. First a trickle, then an absolute deluge of fluttering wings that defied the imagination.

We felt no guilt emulating the Bats as we returned to our bed at 6.30am as they had done one hour previously. Leaving Naracoorte, we took with us some amazing memories, but now Mount Gambia beckoned, and with it—The Blue Lake.

Our late start that morning was of course a direct result of going back to bed after our early morning sojourn in Naracoorte. Once loaded up, we set off with our sights firmly focussed on Mount Gambia and its renowned blue treasure.

I made a brief stop at a BP garage to fill up with petrol and check all the levels before heading for Millicent and the Great Ocean Road. As usual, the roads were almost empty and it was quite something just to see another vehicle. For a second I thought of the UK and its traffic snarl-ups… Driving here was such a joy and holding the wheel with one hand whilst holding her hand with the other was so right.

It was late spring with summer just around the corner and we felt the sun's heat whilst sipping coffee at an outside table in a little restaurant in Millicent. We looked at each other and both leaned forward at the same moment to kiss. For a while we were lost in thought—we were so incredibly fortunate to have found each other. I looked across at her and although she was looking down at the time, she instantly looked my way. "I love you Joan," I said as her hand reached in my direction. I took hold of it. "I love you John, more than you'll ever know." Looking into her beautiful blue eyes, I immediately thought of the Blue Lake. Come on, let's go, we have a rendezvous with one of nature's jewels.

As we departed Millicent, she fell asleep in the car and if she slept for the next two hours, she would awake in Mount Gambia. The radio was playing, so I turned the volume down a little. She must have been tired for she woke just as we arrived at Mount Gambia's outskirts. "Where are we Cookie?" she said. "We're here darling," I replied.

It was now well into the afternoon, so I suggested we go and find some accommodation first. It didn't take long, there were 'vacancy' signs up everywhere and I rather liked the look of the Blue Rock Motel. Joan stayed in the car whilst I went in to check it out. It was perfect, $20 for the night and with a great little café next door for breakfast in the morning.

When talking to the owner about the Blue Lake, she was so helpful and told me it was too late to visit now, but would suggest we leave it until tomorrow and arrive there about noon. Being early November it had already turned blue after the winter period.

"What's the plan Cookie? she said. "Oh it's a fantastic plan," I replied. "We unload our bags and park the car, then we go to our room. We can have a bath, play some nice music, relax and…" "Say no more Cookie, I can see that twinkle in your eye."

She was right of course, and she knew it! I watched television for an hour whilst she was in the bathroom. She had washed her hair and it being so thick took some time to blow dry. When she did finally appear it was worth waiting for—she looked stunning. I disappeared into the bathroom myself—ten minutes later I was out, and made a pathetic attempt at meandering towards the bed.

It was warm and sunny with just a light breeze. The patio doors were ajar but the fly-screens were in place. I put on some soft relaxing music and lay on the bed beside her. She moved slightly and came into my arms, then she put her head on my chest. I touched her long black hair with my fingers. "Cookie," she said. "I'm listening to your heart and it just speeded up!"

"Really," I said, exchanging thoughts of her body for the worst thing I could possibly think of. "How is it now Joan?" I asked. "Still the same," she replied. 'Mmm,' I thought, 'that didn't work.'

I had been waiting ever since we left Adelaide to give her a special present and it seemed now was the perfect moment. I got up, crossed the room and opened my bag. "What are you doing John," she called out. "You'll see in just a moment, I have something for you. Close your eyes, I want it to be a surprise."

"What's this?" she asked, carefully removing the ribbon and wrapping paper without tearing it to reveal a small box. As she lifted the lid, tears rolled down her cheeks at the sight of a gold heart-shaped locket. For a few moments she couldn't speak, not until she had opened it to reveal two miniature photographs of us. "It's so beautiful John, thank you so much – I've always wanted a locket." She slipped it around her neck – it was the perfect length.

Joan was tired and fell asleep quite quickly that gorgeous afternoon, and as she slept I noticed she was still holding the locket with one hand. I sat in a chair on the small patio enjoying the last rays of the sun and I could see her sleeping peacefully through the open door. My mind went back over the past few months. It was difficult to comprehend how much had changed…

It was morning on 21st July earlier this year that the three of us, together with our parents, brother Derek and sister Linda stood at the bus stop close to our home, waiting for the number 128 bus that would take us the half mile to Gordon Hill Station. Here we would catch the train to London and then the underground to Tilbury where the mighty SS *Iberia* was berthed, before transporting us to a new life twelve thousand miles away. Conversation had been minimal – no one knew what to say. All seven of us desperately tried to put on a brave face but failed miserably. For our parents, it was the saddest day of their lives. It was surreal beyond belief and as the train pulled into the station, we said our tearful goodbyes. Our tickets would take us on the first leg of a monumental journey. Not so for the four we were leaving behind, for theirs would only take them no further than the platform.

A tear rolled down my face. I turned my head and looked across the patio to where Joan was fast asleep, still holding the locket…

41

She stirred a little and for one moment I thought she was going to wake up but almost immediately, fell back into a deep sleep once more. The sun had dipped below the horizon and I was aware of a slight change in temperature. For a few seconds I closed my eyes, only to be greeted by her image sitting so forlornly isolated on an empty windswept beach.

With countless thoughts invading my head, I too fell into the arms of Morpheus.

The locket would stand the test of time but at that particular moment, I had absolutely no idea what fate had in store for that small gold heart – or indeed us. Had I been able to 'glimpse the future', I would have seen two old people sitting facing each other in a tea-garden on England's south coast. By their demeanour, it was plainly obvious they had once been close, but with the passage of time had become strangers. There was no physical contact between them, only a 'knowing', an unspoken bond that had prevailed and they communicated simply through their eyes.

The woman slowly reached for her handbag and took out her purse. "No, no – I'll pay," said the old man, slipping his hand into his trouser pocket for some coins. As he did so, she opened a little compartment in the back of her purse and took out a small gold heart and opened it. Passing it to the man, their fingers touching each other's for only the briefest of moments, he could just make out two small faded photographs. His eyes became misty. He blinked in an effort to hold back the tears. He was staring at the locket but she knew he was seeing nothing; he had gone away and was lost in the past…

She broke the silence.

"I've carried your heart with me for a lifetime."

The man didn't speak, he couldn't speak and she knew why.

Mount Gambia and The Blue Lake

We must have been very tired, for we didn't wake up till eight o'clock that evening. "Come on Joan, let's go and have something to eat before everything closes." We got dressed and collected some leaflets on our way out from the reception on Mount Gambia and the Blue Lake. Over two massive burgers, we began to understand why this lake was so special.

It was in fact a large crater in a dormant volcano where the water is a grey steel colour between April and November, then changes to a radiant cobalt blue until March. In a nutshell it's grey in winter and blue in summer. There appears to be two reasons for the colour change which I found very interesting. Firstly, and simply the water temperature, and secondly, the higher position of the sun means more light hits the surface of the lake. This results in increased blue light being scattered out from the lake by small particles.

Divers recently measured the lake's depth which turned out to be seventy-metres. The limestone base may play a part in this conundrum, but the jury is still out on that one. Because the Blue Lake is responsible for Mount Gambia's water supply, nothing is allowed to take place there. It's a shame in one sense but understandable in another, that swimming, boating, and fishing are banned. Break the law and you'll find yourself in deep water!

The following morning after a hurried breakfast we drove full of expectation to take our first glimpse of this amazing spectacle. There were just a few cars in the car park which was about a three-hundred-yard walk from the lake.

Suddenly, there it was, one of those *take your breath away* moments, and we both just stood there as if hypnotised by the colour of the water. It was the bluest blue we had ever seen and cobalt probably summed it up best of all. Amidst the dark vegetation surrounding it, the lake appeared 'alive'. There was little wind that day and barring a few ripples, it was completely calm. It just seemed so out of place here, a jewel that belonged elsewhere.

43

'The Blue Lake'

We sat on a bench, holding hands, not speaking; just looking. It was as if time had stopped for us. Finally, we rose and followed the trail- path that encircled the lake and brought us back an hour later to the car park. As we climbed into our car we were both still a little shell-shocked and couldn't believe what we had just seen. We knew however, that first glimpse of the Blue Lake would stay with us forever.

The Twelve Apostles

The Twelve Apostles

After supper that night, we walked in the town for an hour or so and admired some of the older architecture before returning to the motel for a good night's sleep. Tomorrow we would leave South Australia and head into Victoria for we particularly wanted to visit The Twelve Apostles in the Port Campbell National Park. These limestone stacks have survived for centuries but sadly in January 1990, the one known as 'London Bridge' collapsed.

The whole of the Great Ocean Road is really one big National Park and from Port Campbell we soon had our first view of Victoria's celebrated Stacks—and what a view it was. They certainly lived up to every expectation, a truly phenomenal sight.

Over lunch with a view of the Twelve Apostles, we sat and had a long conversation about several topics. They included her family and what they wanted, the possibility of Hilda meeting someone, would she stay in Australia and how she felt about us and the fact that I was six- years older than Joan. Then there was the question of Tony. What did he want? I know he was fond of Susan Greenwood, but I think she had other ideas.

Joan asked me about my brothers. We'd never discussed what they wanted and where do I really see *us* going. As I said, it was quite a conversation, and very interesting at that. Hilda remained optimistic yet sad inside. Joan doubted her mother would meet anyone after her husband's death.

Tony was an unknown quantity, He was quiet, introverted and it was very difficult to know what he was thinking. At times he was virtually monosyllabic. He had little conversation and seemed to be happy in his own world without unnecessary intrusions.

Garry and Jeff had come to Australia for adventure and to see the world. They knew that in two years they would go home to England. Both were devoid of responsibilities and ties, so they saw Australia as a way out and an opportunity not to be missed. If I'm honest, I felt much the same but I never dreamed I would meet someone so special so quickly—she smiled and gave me a hug.

Our youngest brother Derek had stayed at home with our parents but surprisingly did eventually make the journey to Australia a year after we had returned. He was eighteen months younger than Jeff and went by himself which took a considerable amount of courage.

Derek had worked in the UK for Sotheby's, the auction house and was carving out a promising future for himself. In his spare time he pursued an acting career and had been very fortunate in achieving recognition on National TV and with numerous film parts.

Sadly, in 1997, Derek died from a terminal illness at the age of forty-nine. Our parents, had they been alive would have been devastated. His ashes were scattered over Hampstead Heath, when countless close friends attended the ceremony. They came, not just from the histrionic professions, but from every walk of life.

I wanted to go to Apollo Bay further down the Great Ocean Road but it was a long way and quite close to Melbourne, which in all honesty I wanted to avoid. "I think darling," I said, "we have come as far south as we want to and perhaps it's time to gradually make our way back but by a different route. I've looked at the map and have a good idea where to go." "That's fine with me," she said, so we started back towards South Australia. Little

Derek van Weenen

did we know we would drive through a small town by the name of Penola, where we would learn of an amazing woman, destined for great things.

Sister Mary MacKillip

Sister Mary MacKillip

Purely by chance we arrived in Penola, as Mary MacKillip had done before us. Whereas we came in 1964, she arrived from Melbourne at the age of eighteen in 1860 and took up the position as a governess. It was Father Julian Tenison-Woods who was to have the most profound influence on her life.

He inspired Mary's commitment to the education of all children and lessons were held in a small cottage, St Joseph's Church, and then a stable. Her brother, John MacKillip converted the stable into a proper schoolroom and it was here that the Cradle of the 'Sisters of St Joseph of the Sacred Heart' began. In 1867, she became Mary, Sister of St Joseph and her classes shifted to a purpose-built school building now referred to as the Woods-MacKillip Schoolhouse, which is located on the corner of Petticoat Lane.

Within weeks of the schoolhouse opening, Mary MacKillip boarded the steamship SS *Penola* for the journey to Adelaide, where she went on to establish the Cathedral Hall School, officially took vows and became Mary of the Cross.

The Sisters of St Joseph continued her work in Penola, teaching and living in the schoolhouse off and on until 1889. Later, they established a number of schools and welfare institutions throughout Australia and New Zealand, with an emphasis on education for the rural poor.

The first moves to have Mary MacKillip canonized began in 1926. In 1973, the Vatican allowed Mary to have the title 'Servant of God', which gave formal approval to develop a case for sainthood. She was beatified in 1995 at a ceremony in Sydney during the visit to Australia by Pope John Paul II. In 2009 Pope Benedict XVI approved a second miracle attributed to Mary, which was the final step before she could be declared a saint.

She was canonized in October 2010, during a public ceremony in St Peter's Square at the Vatican and is the first and only Australian to be recognised by the Catholic Church as a saint.

Tailem Bend

Joan was intrigued by Mary's story being a Catholic herself, and surprised at never having heard of her before. Penola, a sleepy little town in the country, was where it all began for Mary and she will always be the town's most famous and special daughter. After lunch at a tiny café and a walk along the main street, we drove away from Penola.

We left with a great deal of reluctance—heading for Tailem Bend.

With just over 100 km to go to Adelaide on the South Eastern Freeway, we reached the railway town of Tailem Bend and decided to stay the night—Aussie style. Perched on the banks of the Murray River it was an old railway community dating back to 1887 when the first Adelaide to Melbourne train came through.

On our left was the Tailem Bend Hotel, a real Aussie pub with a traditional Victorian veranda. Accommodation was inexpensive but adequate as too were their counter lunches.

Tailem Bend Hotel

I left Joan in the car and enquired about a room. "No worries mate," said the barman, "I'll give you a room opening up onto the veranda and with a fantastic view of the railway station." "Thanks,"

I replied. "The Overland to Melbourne will be coming through in an hour and what a sight she'll be for you." It was now seven o'clock and getting dark, so we went to our room—thoroughly delightful for just $10.

"Let's go and have a drink in the bar, there's something I want to tell you." I ordered a schooner of beer and Joan had a glass of wine. "Darling, I want to tell you about my fascination with trains. I have read about Tailem Bend—it's the first stop for the Overland after its left Adelaide and it will be at the station for ten minutes. Maybe we can even go and have a look at the engine." She smiled, but I could see she was not over enthusiastic. "Look around you Joan, look at all this railway memorabilia. There's a drawing of the first train to come through here, seventy-seven years ago."

On every wall were framed pictures of the great steam trains that had once passed through Tailem Bend.

It was 7.55pm. "You're crazy," she said, as we walked hand-in-hand across the road to the small station. "Listen Joan—it's coming." Within seconds the huge diesel train pulled alongside the platform and we walked towards the engine.

"Would you like to come inside the engine?" "NO! Thank you," she replied—I got the message. The driver was leaning out of the window. "How are you?" I said, "I'm good mate, what about you?" "Great thanks, any chance I could come up and see the cab?" "Sure," he said, "mind the steps!" With that I was up and in— "Wow, what a machine!" The two drivers were terrific and explained everything in the time we had. "Well mate, if you don't want to go to Melbourne and leave that little Sheila behind, you better get off," I heard one say.

I thanked them both most profusely and climbed down. They blew the whistle three times and the 'Overland' began to pull away, all four of us waving to each other frantically, like old friends—it was pure theatre, and we all played our part. Within seconds she had gone and only an empty railway line stared back at us.

'The Overland'

Hahndorf

Hahndorf is the oldest surviving German settlement in Australia and we were heading there. It was a different place, like no other, and quite unique. I'm told it was originally settled in 1839 by Prussian Letheran migrants; today it is a thriving community, steeped in wine-growing, with some amazing architecture.

Approaching Hahndorf I could sense Joan was a little sad. "What's wrong darling?" I said. I knew the answer before I'd asked the question. We were coming to the end of our incredible trip and soon we would be home. Without doubt, she would be so happy to see her mother and brother but it was impossible to compare the two. Tomorrow she would be in her own bed—alone, and would miss my face on the opposing pillow as much as I would miss hers.

I thought for a few moments how strange love is. The most powerful feeling in the world, yet when it goes—where does it go to? Love is so strong it can move mountains, yet when one falls 'out of love', and the other person is left 'in love', there is often an overwhelming sense of betrayal or abandonment and loss. To be in love is as close to heaven as you can get in this world.

Scientists on the other hand will offer their formulated theories. They refer to love as a self-induced state of mind, an absolute incarnation of what the individual would like to see and obligingly, the little grey cells comply. I just know, when I look at Joan I am filled with wonder, as I'm sure millions upon millions of people all over the world experience the same feeling about their partners.

As this was the last night of the holiday, I thought it would be nice to stay somewhere different. A public parking area close to the town centre would be a good place to leave the car, soak up the ambience of the town and find some reasonable accommodation. We found it within minutes—an old guest house of German design that had been converted into an hotel. Our room was perfect with quaint little windows looking out over the main street.

The Hahndorf Mill Winery

It had everything we wanted. I spoke to the owners for some advice about wine-tasting tours and a bus was leaving shortly from out front on what he described as the best tour of its kind in Australia.

With the car safe for the night, we climbed aboard an antiquated looking, green open-air bus. The following three-hours flew by and a great talk entitled 'from the grape to the glass', in common with the generous amount of wine consumed, went down extremely well. We arrived back at the hotel, not drunk but not sober, just mildly intoxicated. Joan had a headache, the result of not being used to drinking and tasting so many different wines.

I wasn't far behind her. It was definitely time for a compulsory 'nap' and as in Mount Gambia, we slept till late in the evening.

At nine o'clock and now wide awake, we ventured across the street to an attractive little German restaurant. The meal was first class and with a live-band playing, we danced the night away, assisted by yet more wine. The waiters were most impressed with our selection…

Leaving Hahndorf was sad, for we both knew it heralded the end of our first holiday together. The Stuart Highway wound its way down from the hills through dense forest. Every now and then we'd catch a glimpse of Adelaide far below. An hour later we pulled up outside 91, Sampson Road, the Robinson's home in Elizabeth South. I switched the Zodiac's engine off and she leant across and kissed me. "Thank you so much Cookie, that was the best holiday of my life."

Hilda came rushing out to meet us—tears in her eyes. She was so pleased to see her daughter again. After a nice cup of tea we said our goodbyes. "I'll ring you tonight darling," I said, as I drove out and then onto the Main North Road and headed south. It was a strange and empty feeling that accompanied me on the way back to Henley Beach.

I felt quite alone.

Goliath

Everything was soon up and running at Henley Beach. I found a job with an insurance company, the Temperance and General, in Grenfel Street. Garry went to work in a body shop, and Jeff found employment in a sugar refinery. Then, towards the end of 1964, we received a letter from the estate agents asking us to leave the property, and alarmingly giving us one day's notice. So I went along to see them and asked what the meaning of this letter was.

They explained that the owner wanted his property back. I replied that surely we were entitled to more than one day's notice; we paid by the week after all. The estate agent said that the owner wanted us out the following day. I told them that that was impossible because we hadn't anywhere to go to, and that we needed a week to find somewhere. The estate agent replied that he'd inform the owner, and I went back to tell my brothers.

By the following Friday we were ready to go. We'd cleaned the house, packed up our limited baggage and loaded it into the car. I was in the laundry room overlooking Military road, getting something to eat, as the freezer was kept in there. I was going to cook a steak but it was frozen into the freezer, so I had taken a small hammer and a screwdriver to chip it out.

A car pulled up, and a very tall man about six foot six inches in height, well built, and probably weighed around twenty stones, got out. It transpired he was Polish. Then another three tough looking characters got out of the car. The first chap was so large that he made the men who were with him look small, though they were actually quite sizeable. They came down our pathway into the back garden. Then I heard Garry call out to me. So I went outside, still with the hammer and screwdriver in my hands and asked what the problem was.

Goliath came up close to me. He was aggressive and itching for a fight, a real bully. I looked up at his face, he was massive. "Why

56

are you here, you English scum?" I remember him saying. I told him we were packed up and ready to go that night. I thought all was clear and walked back into the house, but the giant followed me in.

I turned round and he pulled his fist back and swung a punch at my face, fortunately I moved back and his fist went whizzing past. He was angry that he'd missed me, and I ran out into the garden to escape. I felt claustrophobic with that giant near me, and certainly didn't want to aggravate him further.

He followed me out and raised his hands to grab my head. I instinctively raised my hand holding the little hammer and brought it down on his skull. It wasn't a particularly hard blow, but I thought it was enough to stop him, and the blood started to run down his forehead.

I found out later that the hammer had made an indentation in his skull. He stood there frozen for a moment, looking down on me, (I knew how the young David must have felt) and then became *really* mad. He picked up a piece of wood, then I did too, and he came after me. The piece I picked up was triangular.

I hadn't a clue where it came from, but he grabbed the end of it and pulled it out of my hands. Then he swung it and missed me. I ran for our broom that was outside the house and held it by the handle, shouting, "Get back or I'll hit you with this!" He just screamed and charged. He had blood all over his face from the hammer wound by this stage. It was really frightening.

Anyway, as he charged, I was fortunate enough to hit him over the head with the broom, and the handle snapped on his head. I didn't think he could become madder, but then he went berserk, leapt on me and took me to the ground. I couldn't move. Twenty stone pinned me down and he was crushing all the air out of my lungs. I felt panicky, as though I was suffocating. He kept punching me in the face and kneeing me in the stomach and groin.

In the meantime the other men were setting upon my brothers. There was a real punch-up going on, and we were being annihilated. Jeff was only seventeen and, out of the corner of my eye, I saw him get a nasty kick in the groin, which laid him out, unconscious. I was still pinned down by Goliath, trying to avoid his attacks. My younger brother, for whom I felt responsible, was badly injured and I couldn't get to him. I was desperate. Eventually, God knows how, I got clear. I felt very light-headed, my legs were like jelly and I thought I was going to pass out. He came for me again and tried to grab me around the neck, and I knew that if he did, he would strangle me to death.

The house at Henley Beach

In my right hand I still had twelve inches of broomstick left with a sharp jagged end where it had snapped off. As he came for me, I pushed it forward towards his face with all my remaining strength. The blow struck him and lodged into his cheek, penetrating into his mouth. As I did this, I fell and landed at his feet, exhausted and almost unconscious.

I remember looking up and seeing a giant, like Gulliver, towering over Lilliputian me, with this short section of broomstick supported by muscle, gum and teeth, sticking out of his face. He got hold of it and pulled it out. There were spurts of blood that just missed me as I lay there. I rolled away, my eyes were closed and kept rolling. I staggered to my feet and went up the path to try and get help. There was blood everywhere.

I had the orbit bone of my left eye broken, multiple injuries to my body, three cracked ribs and a great deal of pain all over. Some people arrived with the police who were extremely rude, very anti-us, I thought. They believed we were three young, penniless English troublemakers. Perhaps they knew this Goliath? He was a man of means, established, a builder, a New Australian, and successful. I remember one of the policemen came over to us and said, "I don't know where you're going to, and I don't want to know. Just make sure you get out and never come back here."

I found out later why he wanted us out of his house so quickly. During the summer period he could double the rent. He used to let the property out to miners who had spent the winter in the interior of Australia, mainly from Queensland and the Northern Territory.

The Beginning of a Long Journey

We got into the car. I don't know how I drove. I was covered in blood, and my brothers didn't look too good either. We headed for our new accommodation at Semaphore. When we got there we realised that all three of us needed to go to hospital.

We were examined; all had X-rays. I was kept in for two weeks mainly because of my eye, as they wanted to observe any deterioration in eyesight. I was badly bruised in places, especially my testicles, where I'd been repeatedly kneed. I had cuts all over too, where the skin had been taken off. Jeff and Garry were kept in overnight, then allowed home.

All things considered, I felt very relieved I had survived the fight, given the size and strength of my opponent. But lying in hospital, I decided that I couldn't let anything like that happen again. I had felt scared, helpless and impotent.

A week after I left hospital, walking along a street, I saw a yellow estate car go by, and on the roof-rack was a sign that read, 'Learn Karate', and an address in Adelaide. When I was feeling better, towards the end of January 1965, on a Saturday afternoon, I went along to Stuart Street with Jeff.

We found it all right; I think it was called the Australian Judo and Karate Society. From that point onwards, Jeff and I became very serious about karate and trained every day, and I mean every day. We were totally engrossed. *I very much had revenge in mind.*

The *dojo* (training hall) was on the ground floor of a small brick-built warehouse, not in the most salubrious part of the city, more in the industrial sector. Above were offices of some description and access to the *dojo* was via a sliding shutter. It wasn't much but at least we had somewhere to train.

Two-thirds of the *dojo* floor was wooden, the other third being plastic tiling, which was awful once sweat got onto it. It wasn't that large, about sixty feet by forty-five feet, I suppose.

With fellow student Karl Galaish

There were six *makiwara* (striking posts) around the walls, three on one side, three on the other, with carpet pads. The *dojo* seemed to be open most of the time, but Moss Hollis, the instructor, a man of about forty-years of age, worked for a furniture removal business in the daytime.

Training took place during the evening. There were judo and karate classes running simultaneously, but during the time I was there, the numbers in the judo classes decreased, whilst the numbers in the karate classes rose.

The training would go on all evening. Jeff and I would get to the *dojo* about 7.00pm, and we wouldn't stop until about 10.00pm. We'd train for half-an-hour, then take a breather, train for another half-an-hour, and take another breather, and so on. It wasn't as students train today—starting at 8.00pm, finishing at 9.00pm and then off home. In Australia it was much more of a social occasion. During the rest periods, which we needed because the lessons were very demanding and the heat could be really oppressive, we'd stop and take out Nishiyama and Brown's book, *Karate: The Art of 'Empty-Hand' Fighting*, and talk about it, comparing what we'd just practised. We'd ask the senior grades to show us things from the book. I remember asking one high grade to show us *shuto-uke* (knife hand block), which he did, but it was unlike the Shotokan version and we were totally confused. There didn't seem to be a right way, there didn't seem to be a wrong way, it appeared to be *any* way!

Hollis learned his karate from Japanese sailors whose ships arrived, as ours had, at Outer Harbour. Many Japanese ships used to dock, and every other day there was a something or other *maru* in port. The shipping list was advertised in the *Adelaide Advertiser* every week, so we knew where the ships had come from—Kobe, Osaka, and so on. Hollis used to go down to Outer Harbour in his car with the advertisement on the roof-rack, go on board those ships, and ask if anyone knew karate. It didn't matter what style. If any crewmen had trained in karate, and were willing to come when not on duty, he'd pick them up and take them to the *dojo*, which was about twenty miles away. He never paid the Japanese; I think they were just flattered to be asked. We'd give them 'ten out of ten' and buy them a drink afterwards. I think they liked the idea of exporting something from their homeland.

Some of them were brown belts, but a lot were Dan grades (black belts). It was surprising, and a few were very good. I suppose I saw about one hundred Japanese instructors throughout the time I was training at Hollis's *dojo*. But you could never build any kind of relationship with them, as it was a case of 'here today, gone tomorrow'. After training they would be taken back to their ship. Sometimes I took them in my car, but they couldn't speak a single word of English, so that twenty miles was often a bit strained.

In reality, however, we were learning a complete mish-mash, and good Shotokan instruction was rare. Hollis wanted a Shotokan *dojo*, but it wasn't. His three lieutenants were all teaching different things. But Hollis in his own way, was a pioneer.

He was trying to get karate in Adelaide off the ground, learn himself, bring on his own instructors, and keep control of it. We were all thirsty for knowledge. Moss was doing in a much smaller way of course, what Vernon Bell had done in Britain. I remember our badge had a kangaroo on it, (so our jump-kicks should have been first class!).

Moss Hollis is dead now; he died of cancer in the late 1980s. I went back to see him in 1984 and gave him a copy of *The Beginner's Guide to Shotokan Karate*, the first book I had authored on Karate, which hadn't been out long. I recall the great smile that came across his face as he told me that he was proud that one of his students had 'done something'. He seemed to take the full credit for it—I didn't mind.

I had taken my *gi* (karate practice suit) to the *dojo* with me, but I didn't seem to want to train. I don't know why exactly. What they were doing was just so alien, because a lot of water had flowed under the bridge in the intervening twenty years. They weren't training in Shotokan and I just didn't want to get involved. He asked me to teach a class, but I politely refused.

The grading system was devised by Moss and the senior grades based on what was in Nishiyama and Brown's book. When I reached brown-belt, my brothers and I left Adelaide to go walkabout in south-east Australia, with every intention of returning. I'll come back to that later.

I trained at the *dojo* for a year and a half. Hollis graded me throughout. There was an eight *kyu* (learning grade) system in operation, but we kept our white belt and added tags of differing colour to it, which were, if memory serves me right, yellow, green, purple, and brown; then we were awarded the black belt.

About seven months after the fight at Henley Beach, I was walking along King William Street, the main thoroughfare in Adelaide, to where my car was parked. This street was crowded with many people. I could see, about one hundred metres ahead, a man towering above all others walking towards me. It was the Polish giant!

We got closer and closer, and with each and every step forward my heart pounded a little faster, a little louder. The sweat poured from me more profusely. Various scenarios flashed through my mind. Should I bump into him, or just punch him outright? Should I walk straight up to him, or walk past and then turn? Should I follow him to a quieter place? I thought about what people would

63

say to the police. All sorts of things flashed through my mind, and all the time the distance between us shortened.

But then, quite suddenly, I felt a strange confidence come over me. I considered I knew how to fight, though of course I hadn't tried karate out on anyone, but I'd hit the *makiwara* (punching board) thousands upon thousands of times. My knuckles were swollen, I was young and felt strong.

Just before we met, our eyes caught each other's. I could see that something registered in his brain as our eyes seemed to bore into each other's heads. At that moment I just passed him by, almost brushing shoulders as it were, and I never looked back. I knew I could beat him.

I just knew, and all the hate, the revenge I sought after, evaporated. I was just so thankful that I'd found karate. Strangely, one might say, but in some ways I wanted to thank him, because without Goliath, I wouldn't have found karate. No—I never looked back...

The T&G Insurance Company

I was introduced to the T&G through a daughter of some English friends I knew, who happened to know the company was looking for English insurance agents with experience in the field of life assurance. I didn't really want to go back into the same line of work; I hadn't, after all, travelled to the other side of the world to do exactly the same thing I'd tried to escape. However, I didn't have much of a choice, so I put on my suit and tie and trotted off.

I was informed they had a 'Debit' (round) near Henley Beach that had just become available after the retirement of the previous incumbent who'd had it for thirty-years. It sounded nice, I needed the money, and so I took it at a salary of seventeen pounds a week. Unlike my previous less than attractive job of trying to get money from the residents of Camden Town, now I was collecting from middle-class people living in nice houses. They were civilised and relatively affluent, so I decided to try and collect their premiums monthly, thus reducing my workload by three quarters whilst earning the same amount. In truth, it was better all round, causing less inconvenience for everyone. All my clients agreed, so I collected on the first week of the month. The net result was that I worked for two long days and had the next three and a half weeks off. This gave me time to really train in karate and develop my technique. It was a lovely life.

After about three months of this, my supervisor, Geoff Dix, came to see me. He asked how I was getting on, whether I was writing any new business, which of course I wasn't, and said that he'd like to work with me for a few days to see if he could offer any ideas. 'Oh, that's a problem!' I thought, 'that's going to throw a spanner in the works.' Anyway, he came to see me at Semaphore and asked how much I was earning beyond my basic salary in commission. I told him that I wasn't earning any.

This master salesman spent a week with me and I really learned a lot from him. I watched his technique. He was very good indeed but a trifle unorthodox at times.

With Geoff and Lorna Dix

The Finsbury Migrant Hostel

He'd walk up alleyways to look at the washing lines in people's back gardens and gather information. He used this knowledge so that when he knocked on the doors of potential clients, he had a tailor-made policy all worked out in advance. He knew about horticulture and would chat to people about their gardens. After about half-an-hour they'd be old friends, having walked round the property together.

The following week I had a go, and really worked hard, not even stopping for lunch. I even went to bed with my clothes on, I was so worn out. But I didn't write any new business; all I'd done was rush around, without thinking. It was a fruitless week, and it taught me something. So I put on my thinking cap, and tried to think of a virgin patch where no one else had been. I needed a new angle.

Then suddenly, one day, driving past the Finsbury Migrant Hostel, near Port Adelaide, an opening appeared to me. Every week a ship docked carrying migrants from England, and this hostel housed three thousand such people—and none of them had any insurance! But I couldn't gain access; the buildings were fenced off, and there was a large sign saying, 'No hawkers. No salesmen.' I went away, mused, and came up with a plan. I'd join the Good Neighbour Council. I signed up for all the wrong reasons, having an ulterior motive. Helping people didn't enter the equation; I joined solely to take advantage of them. I lied to this voluntary group, and worked for them one evening a week showing a friendly face to newcomers. But what I didn't know then was that this episode was to teach me something of enormous value, and give my life direction more than a quarter of a century later.

Most people who emigrated to Australia had little money, and thought they'd start afresh in a land of milk and honey, but it wasn't like that. The Australian Government kept the passports of those ten pound immigrants for two years whilst they worked. If they wanted to go back home before the two years were up, they had to pay their own fare to the UK, and repay the subsidised amount, less ten pounds. People naturally felt trapped, marooned. I believe there were shades of Australia's past there.

I started showing my smiling, caring face, the mask that hid my *mercenary* intent, at the Glenelg Migrant Hostel. Interesting word *Glenelg*—a palindrome no less (reading the same, forwards or backwards). Before long I had the run of this hostel, and soon I was in the Finsbury Migrant Hostel too. There was a large constant stream of people moving in and out. It was a salesman's utopia.

Something strange however started to happen, because I was beginning to like the voluntary work, and there were some lovely, lovely people there. Joan and I would take a family out for a picnic, or we'd go to the beach on a weekend. I gave them advice on all sorts of things—from paying national insurance to sorting out schools for their children. I fixed them up with jobs. I could have made a fortune. There were so many people and so many avenues for earning commission, but I can honestly say that I never exploited them in any way. I did sell them insurance, but they always asked me for it. I never took advantage of them and I wrote them good, fair policies, and *solely for the breadwinner*.

A Gesture out of Character

I remember one family in particular, but I never knew their surname, although the father's first name was David, his wife's was Margaret, and they had five children. Having just arrived from Hoxton in London, they had some very real problems. David couldn't get a job. He'd been a manual worker in England, but due to the impending Christmas holidays, wasn't going to get a job until February at the earliest. Any employer would have had to pay him over the Christmas and January vacation period.

They had no money, and he was very depressed about the fact. Margaret said to me, "John, we don't want to touch our savings," and I found out that their life savings amounted to barely fifteen pounds. There was no Government benefit, no child support, no one to go to, so it was pretty dire. She told the children that Father Christmas 'wouldn't' be coming that year. I felt really bad about that. It was as genuine a plight as you can get really, and I went out and bought bags of food and boxes of presents for the children. I was single, had money; it wasn't a problem. I knocked on their door and took everything in. They were overwhelmed. She cried, he cried, and the children were jumping up and down with joy. I left them to enjoy the gifts as a family and didn't go back until late January.

I drove away with the most amazing feeling in my heart. I was twenty-four years of age and I think *that was the first really charitable thing I had ever done in my life,* because I wasn't in the habit of giving to help people. My parents hadn't taught me about that kind of thing, and they didn't do it, either. My father just took, because where I grew up you looked after 'number one'.

Once he borrowed five-pounds, a sizeable sum in the fifties, from a local publican. 'Boy' Ede was proprietor of 'The Hop Poles', close to our home and I recall asking my father when he was going to pay this man back. My father said he wasn't going to. I asked him why not, and he retorted that the publican had 'plenty'. I said that he had gone to him cap in hand, 'Excuse me Guv, I can't feed my kids,' and the man had helped. I beseeched him, 'But you promised to pay him back. Haven't you any decency, any pride?' My dad's reply was: 'It's all very well having principles if you can afford to have them.' He never did pay 'Boy' Ede back. I felt very embarrassed, and the memory has stuck with me through the years.

When I did go back to see the family, Margaret had started work locally and was earning a good wage and David had a part-time job maintaining several gardens. All their children had started school and were enjoying it enormously. They very kindly invited Joan and I over for dinner one evening and the children presented us with a present. Words can't explain how touched we were and we will never forget their friendship and hospitality.

The gift they gave us was a picture of a 'Thorn bird', a precursor of things to come in Australia. For years later, in 1983, The Thorn Birds, Colleen McCullough's best-selling novel would be made into a hit mini- series that was shown all over the world.

The Thorn Birds

" T here is a legend about a bird that sings just once in its life, more sweetly than any other creature on the face of the earth. From the moment it leaves the nest it searches for a thorn tree, and does not rest until it has found one. Then, singing among the savage branches, it impales itself upon the longest, sharpest spine.

And, dying, it rises above its own agony to out sing the lark and the nightingale. One superlative song, existence the price. But the whole world stills and listens, and God in His heaven smiles. For the best is only bought at the cost of great pain...

Or so says the legend."   *Colleen McCullough*

*Meggie Cleary and
Ralph de Bricassart*

I had always enjoyed the 1983 Australian mini-series 'The Thorn Birds', a story of forbidden love between Father Ralph de Bricassart played by Richard Chamberlain and Meggie Cleary, portrayed by Rachel Ward.

In the early scenes of 'The Thorn Birds', Meggie was a pretty *eleven-year-old* girl and the child actress, Sydney Penny, performed the demanding role superbly. A lone child, brought up in the Outback at Drogheda, a vast sheep station in northern New

South Wales in the 1920s. Sadly ostracised by many and blatantly neglected by her mother, she remained a forlorn figure—that was until the arrival of Father Ralph...

Four-years prior to 1983 when 'The Thorn Birds' was released, I was living in the village of Clophill in Bedfordshire where I had just built a swimming pool. My intention was to teach swimming and after qualifying, set about creating the 'Hilltop Swimming Club'.

Eleven-year-old Meggie

One Sunday morning, John and Yvonne Speller enrolled their *eleven-year-old* daughter in one of my beginner's classes. Hannah was bright, attentive and within a month, was swimming the length of the pool unaided. She was a delightful girl with perfect manners and soon became one of my best pupils. She attended classes for a couple of years, during which time her parents and I became good friends.

In 1981, I sadly lost touch with the Speller family and never saw them again.

Hannah Speller

On 2nd July 2018, I was walking along the pavement in my home town of Olney in Buckinghamshire, when a woman suddenly stopped in front of me. "Hello John," she said, "it's me—Hannah." It took a few moments to register who she was, after all —I hadn't seen her for thirty-seven-years.

It was wonderful being reunited with her after all this time and she came to my house and we talked for ages.

Sadly her father had died in 1998 and her mother never remarried. She passed-away in 2016 and surprisingly, had lived only a few miles from Olney. Hannah was married and living with her husband and two girls in Sydney, Australia, but was in England now to meet the lawyers and sort out her mother's belongings.

The list of coincidences were quite amazing. I had gone to Australia some years before she had, yet we were destined to rendezvous almost forty-years after we had last seen each other. Little Meggie was *eleven-years-old* when she appeared in 'The Thorn Birds' and Hannah was *eleven-years-old* too, when she came to learn to swim.

To cap it all, when I looked at Hannah standing there in front of me, there was a distinct likeness between her and Rachel Ward, as she is today. Hannah smiled at me for she knew exactly what I was thinking, having sometimes been mistaken for the star in Sydney, where Rachel lives also.

Meeting Hannah after so many years was an amazing coincidence—or was it?

My thoughts went back to 1993 when I first read James Redfield's 'The Celestine Prophecy', with its overriding message: *'There's no such thing as coincidence'.*

Rachel Ward

Guard Against Impetuous Courage

About six months later, Mr Dix called on me again, and brought the news that I had underwritten more business than all the other twelve hundred and forty agents in the firm throughout the whole of Australasia, bar one. Dix was as the proverb says, 'over the moon'. I'm not proud of my purpose, my intent in attending that hostel, but I am proud of the fact that I could do business honestly, where everyone was a winner. I learned a lot, and really liked this new-found feeling of giving as well as taking.

Before I move on, however, I'd like to relate a story that happened at Semaphore Beach. My brothers and I had rented a flat on the esplanade. The two boys from next-door, Hughie and Alan, joined us at the annual fair and we had rides on the dodgems and other amusements. Standing beside one particularly stomach-churning affair called the 'Chair-o-Plane', that went up and down and round and round, was a young couple in their late teens waiting for their friends, who were having fits of laughter on the ride. My companions and I walked past, and coming towards us was a group of youths, a gang, and they were the sort of gang you see in the movies—the kind you take an instant dislike to. There were about twenty to twenty-five of these good-for-nothings, and as they walked along they were kicking things, throwing bottles and generally trying to pick a fight with anyone they saw. They were mainly Italian and Greek, each dressed in black leather with studs, and all had tattoos—they were like the archetypical motorbike gang, but minus bikes.

As soon as I saw them my hackles went up, because these New Australians were out for trouble. The leader of the gang was swaggering along, and saw the couple up against the fence. He veered off from his mates and walked up to them. Grabbing hold of the boy, he spun him around and punched him on the nose. This young man's nose broke, smashed to a pulp, and as he fell to the floor his screaming girlfriend tried to catch him. The leader of the gang turned to his mates, who cheered, and I just saw red. I couldn't control myself; quite stupidly really, because we could have been annihilated. As the leader walked back, and it sounds corny now, and it certainly isn't me, I shouted, "You bastard. Why don't you pick on someone your own size?"

The leader turned, looked at me and called back, "Oh, so you want some as well do you?" He started to walk very slowly towards me, and as he did so, one of his mates moved out and round to my left, as though to out-flank me. It looked as if there was going to be a real punch-up. I leapt into a kind of freestyle stance with my left foot slightly in front of my right, which was something you just didn't see in those days—karate was virtually unheard of. The leader moved close as if he was going to get hold of me and I was watching him.

Out of my peripheral vision, I could make out one member of his gang to my left, closing in, approaching me rapidly.

As this yob to my side was about to attack, I let fly with an *uraken* (backfist-strike) and it struck him on the temple. He went down as if hit by a bullet; knocked out, unconscious. The strike was spot on. I never really even looked at him because I was concentrating on the leader. When his crony fell, the leader muttered, "That's karate!" turned, and sauntered off, some of his mates carrying the unconscious friend I'd laid out. I find it embarrassing telling the story, but it's all true.

When the gang walked away, Alan and Hughie were agog. "Where did you learn that!" they asked, but one of my brothers turned, shook his head, and dampening any immediate euphoria I might have enjoyed, and in an unbelieving voice commented, "You must be f***** mad! They could have killed us!" and I replied, "Yes, but they didn't, did they?" Master Funakoshi's maxim, '*Guard against impetuous courage*' didn't mean too much to me in those days! But I knew I'd been lucky. We went over to the young man who had been punched, put him in the car, and took him and his girlfriend to hospital. His face was swollen; it was nasty.

I'd been training hard since I had been attacked by the Pole and suddenly here was another real-life case. When the young man had been hit, it was as if the giant had hit me, and now I could do something about it. I felt that an injustice had been righted, and it felt really good. Although I must have hurt this thug, though I never did find out what his injuries were, I can't say I lost much sleep over him. But there was one incident over which I *did* lose sleep.

Jeff's Close Call with Davey Jones

At weekends, my brothers and I loved to go surfing; Joan always came with us but insisted on remaining a spectator. She found our surfing antics amusing, especially when we fell off the board more than we stayed on it (which usually happened). When we weren't working or training, we were surfing. We used to listen to the surf report each weekday morning on local radio and if conditions were good, with an offshore breeze, we'd get up at 5am, jump into the car, and off we'd go to Moana Beach, which was about an hour's drive from our new apartment in Semaphore.

There were good waves at Moana, not too big, six or seven feet, and if you caught one, you had a nice ride in. On one particularly hot Sunday we went to Moana and spent the whole day there. The sky and sea were a beautiful blue, the waves were building up, so Garry and Jeff decided to go out. Joan and I relaxed on the beach together with a couple of cold Cokes and watched the boys. They paraffin waxed their boards—the wax helps your feet to grip—and set off.

Jeff had gone out quite a way to where the waves began to build—Garry was a little closer to us. To our delight, Jeff caught a wave beautifully and, standing up on the board, rode the wave past his brother in our direction. As the wave increased in height, poor Jeff fell off and disappeared under the water.

In the meantime, Garry had caught a wave himself and surfed past Jeff in undeniable style. From our vantage point on the beach it was obvious Jeff was in big trouble, he was floundering and drowning. He told us later he was shouting help as Garry passed him but the noise of the breaking waves was deafening and he didn't hear him.

I grabbed my board and paddled out as fast as I could in Jeff's direction. There was one big wave between us that was about to break so I turned the board over, submerged myself and held on

77

tight. As it passed, I righted myself and paddled furiously to Jeff and pulled him onto the board.

He was still conscious but had obviously swallowed a lot of water as the waves brought us in to the beach. Other surfers came over and gave him assistance after which, covered in towels, he was violently sick before falling asleep. Half an hour later he woke up and amazingly, was as right as nine-pence! I think we all said a silent prayer that day.

Sharks

O n another occasion that I will never forget, an incident happened at Noarlunger Beach. Garry and I had paddled out about a quarter of a mile and waited for the right wave to come. I can feel the salt spray on my mouth now. I heard the sound of an engine in the distance but thought nothing of it, and looked up to see a light plane coming towards us at a very low altitude. This aircraft was used as a shark spotter and patrolled the beaches.

It flew towards us coming closer and closer, and then banked steeply and began to fly in circles above our heads. The noise was quite deafening. 'Jesus!' I thought, 'we're sitting on top of sharks!' I was absolutely petrified. I scrambled onto my board and pulled in any bits that normally hung over.

I shouted out to Garry, "Get onto your board quickly—there are sharks in the water!" As I lay there praying, an enormous black shadow passed right under my surfboard—I'm sure it was a Great White (shark). I called out, "Christ! There's one here!"

Then the wave we'd been waiting for came. I paddled briefly, put my arms back onto the board, and let the wave take me. I was in dire straits though, because I couldn't spread my weight in my normal standing fashion. We went into shore lying down, and that taught me a lesson about balance that I've never forgotten.

That close call frightened the life out of me and I didn't go back into the water for quite some time. It took me a while to get over it, because if I'd lost my balance I could easily have been eaten alive. It makes me shudder to think of it and sometimes I break into a cold sweat as my memory flashes back to that incident at Noarlunga Beach.

...and John is wearing swimming trunks.

Gone on The Ghan

F inally, my commission came through from work after coming 2nd in the T&G's National competition and to my absolute delight, a cheque for £2,000 was staring me in the face. I'd promised the boys if it was 'sizable', I would take them on a special trip for a few days. Watching me open the T&G envelope, both immediately saw the expression of delight on my face and expected me, (using true colloquial Aussie), to *come good*. "Where are we going to?" They both asked at the same time. I had to tell them.

"We're going on The Ghan, and we'll be leaving on Thursday morning, providing I can get the tickets." They were ecstatic. They knew of the train but not a great deal about it, so over dinner I explained a little of its history as one of the world's great train journeys.

"The Ghan leaves Adelaide every Tuesday and Thursday and covers the 1500 kilometres to Alice Springs in twenty-four hours. I've always wanted to go on this train ever since school days when I first read about it. The Ghan travels over the salt-bush-plain of South Australia and runs close to The Flinders Ranges. I remember reading about 'The Old Ghan' which used to follow the famous narrow gauge track to Alice Springs through these mountains. The journey took three days, if you were lucky. Floods, rockfalls, sun-buckled rails and so on would often delay the old Ghan, but then the passengers would have a party. Today, she is still remembered as an Australian legend.

"The new Ghan travels on a recent standard all-weather gauge track. I remember having it explained to me that the name 'Ghan' comes from the Afghan or 'Ghan' cameleers who transported goods and I believe people too, by camel train throughout the arid Outback."

"Can't wait," said Jeff, "and best of all, we've got a freebie!" "Don't worry, Captain, you both deserve it," I replied. Jeff's nickname was Captain Morgan, but had been shortened to Captain.

Two days later we presented ourselves at the Adelaide Rail Passenger Terminal, the long silver grey train quivered, then pulsed gently into motion. Pulled by two streamlined diesel electric engines, in the green and gold livery of the Australian National, we began to glide north. Adelaide unfurled past our windows. We were on our way.

There are many stories in circulation about the old Ghan but this one is almost a legend. It tells of a woman on the Ghan who keeps asking the conductor what time they get to Alice Springs. Every time the train stops she asks him. The conductor gets a little impatient. "What's the hurry?" He says. "We'll get there some time in the next few days." So the woman says, "Listen, I'm due to have a baby." "Well," says the conductor, "You shouldn't have got on the train in this condition." And the woman says: *"When I got on the train, I wasn't in this condition."*

I guess the Aussies are quite nostalgic when it comes to the old Ghan.

It wasn't possible to get a cabin for three, so Garry and Jeff shared a 'Twinette' and I had my own. Being the first time we had been on such a train it was very exciting. Each cabin had two pull-down beds, a private shower and toilet, and a big picture window; an impressive concentration of comfort and convenience and in such a small area. As the Ghan sped through the South Australian countryside, we couldn't help but recall the latest James Bond movie, *From Russia with Love* which had been released the year before. The comparison between the Venice Simplon Orient Express and the Ghan was obvious. Perhaps it was my imagination but Garry seemed to be viewing some of the other passengers with a certain amount of suspicion!

This was an amazing train and the Ghan was hurtling along with an absolute minimum of noise and fuss. We sat together in my cabin with a feeling we had been launched into space, watching South Australia pass by on a big television screen.

The boys went off to explore the rest of the train leaving me with my own thoughts. Joan was uppermost in my mind and despite her lack of enthusiasm with the 'Overland' at Tailem Bend, I was sure she would love the Ghan and I made a commitment mentally to take her on it at some point.

I wandered along to the lounge car with its piano, bar and armchairs and talked to several people. They were all very friendly and there seemed to be a holiday atmosphere prevailing. I met an eighty-seven-year-old man called Jim. He was 'full of beans', sprightly and a long way from popping-off. He was travelling on his own, came from Queensland and would join a coach party at Alice Springs for the Red Centre tour—amazing.

Three hours after leaving Adelaide, the Ghan slid into Port Pirie and paused for an hour. We got off and stretched our legs. On one side the Port Pirie skyline is dominated by what I think are grain silos and on the other, the Flinders Ranges. We walked into the town. It was hot, dusty and slow paced after the big city bustle of Adelaide. Quite honestly, we were all conscious of the time and not being left behind.

Then we sped on to Port Augusta, a likable old town and a half hour stop. The relaxed attitudes induced by rail travel presumably were apparent again on the platform. There were none of the tensions of an airport departure lounge here. We ambled about, chatted and bought picture post cards. The conductors kept a benign eye on us to make sure we got back on board in time. It was good to come out of the heat to the cool comfort of our now familiar cabins.

The Ghan galloped on. Now we were, according to one old chap, in Mulga country. I knew about this hard, tough acacia wood from my visit to an Aboriginal settlement with Joan, where we had watched it carved and shaped into boomerangs. As the horizons flattened out, the land seemed empty of humanity, houses and animals. It was immensely barren and desolate.

To an eagle—and apparently many eagles soar across these enormous skies—the Ghan must look like a long silver millipede scurrying over an endless plain.

Captain and I had lunch together as Garry was occupied with a rather pretty looking Aussie girl and they appeared to be getting on like a house on fire. We later found out her name was Pamela and she was going home to Alice Springs. We drank to his good fortune with some fine Moselle wine. When we boarded the Ghan we were each given a precise map of the train's route and it was interesting and quite enjoyable following it.

Now we were really in the Outback and we pelted through lonely railway townships like Pimba and Kingoonya as nature began to prepare for a glorious sunset. Captain really got into his map-reading and knew exactly where we were and what was coming up next.

Occasionally we would see the odd kangaroo and mostly the view we saw was of its backside scuppering away from the train. The sun was low in the sky which in the west was turning ever more red. An incredible sunset was imminent. Over the loudspeaker, in a really broad Australian accent, it was announced that dinner would be served in one hour. Enough time for a shower, change of clothing and completing the wine order.

The roast beef was succulent and beautifully prepared and accompanied by a very good claret. Through the double-glazed window we watched the sun dip below the horizon to form the most beautiful backdrop of reds and oranges I have ever seen. It was quite mesmerising.

Two hours later we adjourned to the lounge car; the folks on the next table joined us and there was a great friendly, country atmosphere. A lady began playing the piano and everyone starting singing. The waiters were first class and the drinks kept coming. We had never experienced anything like it and all the time we were speeding through the night, crossing the mighty Outback and drawing closer with every mile to Alice Springs.

We slept well that night, very well. After breakfast as we finished packing, the Ghan slid through Heavitree Gap, past some Aboriginal houses where black people waved and watched and past the rocky walls of the MacDonnells, till there she was—*The Alice.*

'The Alice' and the MacDonnell Ranges.
Echo's of Neville Shute's famous novel, 'A Town Like Alice'.

John Spencer, a tour guide who had been recommended to me was there to meet us at the station. He drove us to a small hotel and after checking in, left with a promise to return at five o'clock that afternoon. It was then I told the boys about my surprise.

"John is a guide with special knowledge of the Aboriginal way of life. He'll collect us at five and drive us out to a small station he owns. From there he'll saddle up four horses and take us into the bush where we'll spend the night under canvas. He'll cook Aboriginal tucker over a camp fire and he guaranteed me, we would find it delicious. In the morning, he will bring us back to the hotel about eight o'clock where we can wash and maybe sleep, before picking us up at noon in time to catch our flight back to Adelaide."

Garry looked at Jeff, they were speechless. "Wow. What can we say. What a fantastic experience. Thank you."

John was waiting for us at 5.00pm and we jumped aboard his station waggon. Half an hour later we had left *The Alice* behind and arrived at his property. It was obvious he had done this many times before as everything was ready to go. All he had to do was saddle the horses and in no time we had mounted and were on our way, to God knows where. An hour later we arrived at a stream which we crossed and made camp under some huge gum-trees. It was approaching twilight and he got to work erecting the tents, which he did in no time. We offered to help but he preferred to do it himself. Thirty minutes later, he had erected two tents, kitted them out and had a roaring fire on the go. We felt a little superfluous.

The western sky was a brilliant orange, it was so peaceful here save for the sound of the crickets. Stars began appearing in the evening sky and he produced a table and some chairs from nowhere. John was amazing, so professional. The horses were taken care of, dinner was cooking and we felt quite guilty not being allowed to help in any way.

"Dig in," he said, "just help yourself." We did and the food was delicious. He produced some white wine which appeared to come out of the stream. It was cold and he gave us a bottle each. It was an incredible evening and after dinner he told us stories all relating to this area and *The Alice*. We thought about it but didn't ask him what we had just eaten, we unanimously decided it would be in our best interest to remain ignorant.

John was so knowledgeable and he talked about the Aborigine culture and even recited their poems. Eventually he suggested we might 'hit-the-sack' as he could see we were 'dropping off'. We thanked him so much and before we retired, he gave us a quick five-minute tour of the night sky. We recognised the southern cross but that was about it.

We all slept like logs only to be woken in the morning by the smell of bacon cooking over the camp fire. It certainly smelt like bacon but again decided to not ask silly questions. It was however very tasty and we recognised eggs when we saw them. But, they were too small for chicken's eggs...

The ride back to his place in the early morning was invigorating to say the least, but memorable. From there it was back to our hotel. He said he would come for us at noon and run us to the airport which he did. It was very sad saying goodbye to John and we just stood there watching his pick-up truck disappearing in a cloud of dust.

Our flight back to Adelaide was uneventful and within three hours or so, we were in a cab heading for Semaphore. That night, we would all sleep in our own beds but our thoughts would be back there, a thousand kilometres away, under the stars, with a man we hardly knew, and who we probably would never meet again.

Andamooka

S peaking of sweating reminds me of another story! I've always had a fascination with opals. There are different kinds: milky-white, or bluish with yellow, green and red reflections, some forms of which show changing colours, and they appear to be alive as this is split and reflected by the silica molecules. I often looked in the jewellery shops in Adelaide, and really wanted to buy a stone for my mother.

One morning before breakfast, I got up and browsed through the *Adelaide Advertiser*. There, in headlines on the front page was a story of three fourteen-year-old schoolboys who had gone up to the opal mines at Andamooka, struck it rich, brought their opals back and sold them to a dealer for ten thousand pounds, which then was an extremely large sum of money.

The story caught my imagination, and I said to Jeff and Garry, "Look at that!" So Garry suggested, "Let's have some of that. Let's just go!" Jeff agreed, but I continued, "Hang on a minute. We don't know anything about opal mining!" However, we were determined to make our fortune. We weren't going to take our mother back an opal; we were going to present her with a lucrative opal mine!

I went to the local library and took out everything I could find about opals and geology. We learned that opals are found in cracks in igneous rocks, under what we called green stone. I went to the hardware shop and bought opal picks, buckets, ropes, helmets, candles and so on—everything needed to go opal mining. We spent eighty-five pounds on equipment. Then I went to the ministry office and got three 'Miners Rights' to dig in South Australia, which cost five shillings (25p) each. I also bought three large containers to hold water, because where we were going there wasn't any. We loaded up the Zodiac and off we went!

We drove north to Port Pirie, in the Spencer Gulf, then further north, until we came to a dust track that was signposted to Andamooka. Arriving at the mining fields, two huts greeted us, and we were shortly to learn that the miners lived underground, like cavemen, because of the searing heat. It was 135° Fahrenheit (57.2 Celsius) in the sun and over 100°F (40°C) in the shade. It was a mining settlement; there were no policemen and you were on your own; it was just a frontier town and you had to be careful. There were only sheds, and holes in the ground. Nowadays, in some opal mining towns, there are shops, churches, and even hotels located underground.

When we arrived, we stopped the car outside a shed that had a sign saying, 'Ben Cogshill'. We went in and met him. He was the classic Aussie gouger (opal miner), thickset and unshaven—a man's man. The first thing I said to him, like a naïve Pommie was, "Good day! How are you?" and he replied, "Bloody hot! What sort of stupid question is that?" Like a fool, I then asked him an equally foolish question. "Can you tell me where we might dig for some opals?"

He looked at me incredulously, and retorted, "Are you f****** mad! I've been up here looking for thirty-two years, if I knew where the f****** things were do you think I'd still be here?" I said, "Sorry Mr Cogshill, but we're up here and we'd like to have a go."

He pointed us in the direction of an area known as 'German Gully', and gave us a cup of water that we shared. The sweat was pouring from us, and I drank the first third.

It was so incredibly hot. Taking only a few steps was exhausting. Arriving at German Gully we began to search for the elusive green stone, looking for undulations in the strata. Any exposed deposits meant that we didn't have to dig too deeply to find the opals. We found the green stone, looked around and put pegs in the ground to stake our claim. We had to exercise extreme caution, not wanting to encroach upon anyone else's claim. If you claim-jumped out here, you'd get shot and buried in that searing wilderness. No one would ever find you.

After three hours digging, we had drawn a blank, and decided to try elsewhere. I discovered an old working on a ridge nearby, so we filed our claim around this deep hole, which was about four-feet wide and sixty-feet deep. I went down first. There were handhold steps, but I had to be careful, and was roped up. When I got to the bottom, it opened up into a cave on one side where former miners had dug, and it was relatively cool. All the equipment was sent down. The water was almost boiling; we couldn't drink it and we had to lower it carefully down the shaft and place it in the cave so that it would cool down. The candles, four dozen of them, had melted into one lump. We had one giant candle with forty-eight wicks sticking out of it! I had to cut slices off like a cake, and we ended up with triangular candles.

For safety's sake, we needed to take precautions because we were in a confined and insecure space. If all three of us had been working down in the cave, any madman could have come along and buried us, so we always had one person up above by the car as a precaution, whilst the other two dug.

We chiselled away expectantly and started to find little chips of opal, which sparkled green and red in the candlelight. Jeff became really excited. As I worked, I dreamed that when I got back home I'd walk into some fancy showroom and pay cash for a new E-type Jaguar convertible. We became filthy, but couldn't wash—water was strictly for drinking. Sleep was impossible up above in the tents because of the damned mosquitoes, and those insects were bad news. We couldn't sleep in the car at night because it retained the day's heat and acted like an oven.

It was terrible and all three of us suffered from sleep deprivation. The conditions were appalling. We had to lift every scrap of the chipped rock out in a bucket in that incredible heat. All that effort to acquire semi-precious stones created from silica suspended in water!

The cave ceiling was very low and we worked doubled-up or on our stomachs. At night, that heavy ceiling seemed to taunt us with the prospect of crushing the life out of us if we ever let our guard drop. In a sense, a very real sense, as we chipped away we were making a tomb for ourselves.

Two very hot, would-be 'Gougers' in the Australian
Outback. With no police or law and order at Andamooka, it
was every man for himself.
Here, Garry with his .22 rifle, the very essence of vigilance,
was in charge of dealing with 'claim jumpers' who
took a liking to our pitch. Fortunately, his trigger finger
remained redundant!
An Adelaide cell had little appeal.

It was claustrophobic, and my mind, almost in a state of delirium, journeyed back twenty-years to my childhood when the basement living room in Canonbury Road Enfield became a bedroom fitted with a Morrison air-raid shelter. This shelter was a bolted-up steel double bed with a built-in thick steel sheet that covered the entire structure. Getting into bed was not easy, with only two feet clearance between the sheets and the bed's iron roof. Despite being only three years old, I could recall countless occasions lying in that bed, sandwiched between my parents, staring up at the steel sheet, and listening to the V1 *doodlebug* flying bombs.

The feeling of claustrophobia inside that wartime bed was acute. I felt pinned down, trapped, and unable to move in the pitch dark. The silence was broken only by the eerie throbbing of the pilotless projectiles as they flew overhead. Suddenly, the noise would stop and seconds later you'd hear an explosion that would rattle the windows. Many a night I sobbed myself to sleep, and although my parents tried to pacify me, they too were anxious and exhausted.

We were digging away one day, when we just stopped, looked at each other, and, without saying a word, packed up and left. All we could think about was the ocean, and swimming.

The sun and the heat were beginning to have an effect on our minds. I could feel myself beginning to *lose it*, becoming almost demented at the thought of lying in the cool, clear blue sea, and having a beer straight from the fridge. So we left Andamooka—without a single opal.

Writing to our parents in England the previous month, I had promised my mother I would bring her back an opal ring. Not wanting to disappoint her, on arriving back in the UK two years later, I took myself off to Hatton Garden in London. There I bought the opal pictured here, had it made into a ladies ring and presented it to her from the three of us. She must have known we hadn't found it in Australia but never let on.

She was thrilled and wore it almost constantly until her death in May 1982. When her Will was read out, I discovered she had one final surprise for me. She had left me her opal ring with a little note. "I loved this ring and each time I looked at it, I was reminded of you Garry and Jeff and your kindness. It's yours now John, and I would like you to have it made into a gent's ring and perhaps, when you look at it, it may remind you of me." I carried out her wish—it's above—and it does.

The nearest town was Woomera, which was a British and Australian top-secret centre for rocket and guided-weapon research and, like Andamooka, was in the proverbial 'middle of nowhere'; outsiders weren't allowed in there. It had been built in the late 1940s and I said to my brothers, "Let's see if we can get in." Had we known of the radiation threat that would affect many in years to come, we would not have gone, We drove for about four hours. The road was terrible—all potholes and boulders and soft sand.

We'd driven two thousand miles across the desolate Nullarbor Plain to Perth the year before, but this road was something else. We got stuck in the sand a few times and had to push the car out, but eventually arrived at Woomera about six o'clock in the evening, totally exhausted.

Black Opal

Approaching the barrier, which was guarded by soldiers, we explained our plight. I told them we'd been mining, had no food or water and needed to get supplies as a matter of urgency; all of which was true. We were in a bit of a mess. The guard rang through and came back with the message that we had three hours to get all we needed. After searching the car and us, they signed three-hour passes. It was made quite clear that if we didn't leave by nine o'clock, we'd be locked up.

We drove into the town and came to the swimming pool. I slammed the brakes on, and we leapt out of the car leaving all the doors wide open, ran past the woman in the kiosk, taking our clothes off as we ran, and dived into the water. The lifeguard came over and was sympathetic; then we got out of the pool and went back to the car, picking up our discarded clothes as we went. A restaurant was next on our list. We ordered a nice big meal and some cold beers. Those beers went down just like in that famous scene with John Mills, Harry Andrews, Anthony Quayle and Sylvia

Syms in the film, Ice Cold in Alex. We had a limited stroll round, though it was mostly a case of avoiding restricted areas. However, we did speak to a couple of scientists we met on our way round.

Nine o'clock found us at the barrier again, and we returned our passes. I explained to the guard that we had nowhere to go, and that we were worried about pitching our tent in the desert, so they let us camp by their hut, and we had a good night's sleep with a soldier guarding us. The following day we drove back to Adelaide, empty-handed—though 'empty' doesn't mean 'nothing' does it? (*Kara-te*, empty-hands). Our adventure had been rough and it had been tough, but we were living a different kind of life, and it was real.

When it was time to leave Adelaide to 'go walkabout' (a term of Aboriginal origin), Jeff, Garry and I got into my car and drove to Melbourne in Victoria and then up to Sydney in New South Wales. We moved into a modest hotel called Bondi Lodge, close to the world-famous Bondi Beach. Sydney, which had a population of over two million people at the time, was Australia's largest city, and the centre for karate in Australia.

I'm Forever Blowing Bubbles

Positions were advertised for people to work on an early form of automatic car-wash, and Jeff and I applied. We arrived at the designated garage at 7.30am in the Sydney suburb of Rushcliffe, and stood outside, not quite sure what to do. There were about ten other men waiting. In front of us was the car-wash. A dirty car would be driven onto a conveyor belt, and would move very slowly round in a large arc. By the time the arc was completed, the fourteen or so men standing either side of the vehicle would have the vehicle sparkling.

There were seven pairs and each man stood opposite his partner, with each pair having a specific job. The men remained stationary as the car moved past, but they had to work quickly. The foreman pointed to Jeff and me, and we were directed to put overalls on. Jeff was my partner and our job was to get the dirt from the car, from one bumper to the other, wearing two large mitts each, after it had been sprayed with water. Things were constantly going wrong. The conveyor belt was too fast so the machinery would break down. It was very stressful, and all the time there were other men outside waiting to take our jobs.

The foreman, who was really foul-mouthed and unpleasant, sacked people left, right and centre. Constantly shouting and swearing; he had a real problem. We started work at 8.00am and the cars were going through at such a pace, it took four-minutes or so to clean each car; it was non-stop.

We'd been training in karate, but our arms were nearly dropping off after hours of this, and we needed a rest. Suddenly, the conveyor belt stopped and the foreman shouted at me, "Come here! Look at that. You've missed that bit! I told you to f*****g well clean the car. If you do that again, you're out!" "Look, we've done twenty or thirty cars. It's tiring," I replied. "If you do it again, you're out," he shouted.

"Sorry," I said, indignantly, and the conveyor belt was switched back on. Jeff and I soaped our mitts and off we went again. About ten minutes later, the conveyor belt stopped abruptly, and the foreman looked across at Jeff.

"Come here!" he bellowed at the top of his voice. All the others were looking at the foreman and thinking, 'You bastard.' Anyway Jeff, who was smaller than me, had missed the glass on a driving mirror, and the foreman grabbed Jeff by his overalls and shouted, "Clean that f*****g car properly!" The atmosphere was grim; the foreman turned to me becoming very agitated as I walked in his direction saying,

"What did you say?"

"Don't f*****g talk to me," he retorted, "or you're out!"

"We're going," I answered.

He became aggressive and walked towards me in a threatening manner, invading my space, and I hit him as hard as I could in the face with a right *uraken* (back-fist-strike), wearing this huge mitt, before he could hit me. He went down, drenched, and covered in soap. As he got up he was blowing bubbles as he tried to blaspheme, and everyone on the site was laughing, clapping and cheering, because he'd got his comeuppance.

"Right!" He spluttered and shouted, "What are you looking at!" I'd had enough and I answered him back.

"Actually, I'm looking at you," I replied. He didn't like that at all.

"Don't you f*****g well look at me unless I tell you to," he screamed.

He appeared to be understandably deaf in one ear, as my blow had contacted his right temple.

"What's your name?" and I told him.

He staggered over to the clocking machine, found my card, and clocked me out, about ten times. He went berserk, and took his frustration out on the machine. I felt a bit sorry for it—the machine that is. Jeff and I took our overalls off, it was 10.30am and I asked for our money for the two and a half hours we had worked.

"Come back on Friday," he shouted, and with a wave to the other guys we left. We never did go back though—you never know, he might have had some of his pals waiting for us.

So the situation was quite grim. We had no money, couldn't get work and our car stood forlornly in the kerb outside Bondi Lodge with an empty fuel tank. It seemingly couldn't get any worse.

Sheer Greed

Every Wednesday, jobs were advertised in the *Sydney Morning Herald*, and at that time, work was very scarce. I managed to get a position as a night-porter in the Hotel Charles at Bronte, a seaside resort a couple of miles away from Bondi.

The resident chef was a rather uncommunicative Frenchman by the name of George who ruled the kitchen with a rod of iron. He was known disaffectionately as 'King George' by the kitchen staff, but despite his unfriendly manner, he apparently was an extremely accomplished chef who had worked at Maxim's in Paris.

The second chef, a-dyed-in-the-wool Aussie suggested to me I should give 'King George' a wide berth. "Why's that," I asked. He stopped what he was doing and looked up at me, his eyes narrowed. "Because he hates the English," he replied. "What have I done to him?" I said. "Nothing mate," came the answer. "Just don't do anything wrong or he'll have your guts-for-garters." With that, he quickly went back to his chopping board. His anxiety was palpable.

George didn't have a pastry chef at the Bronte Charles so that duty had to be shared. I had previously tasted a piece of one of George's apple pies—it was delicious, and one evening during my break, I watched him making one. He always made them in rectangular trays measuring two feet by one foot. By the time my fifteen-minute break had finished, I had learnt his secret and immediately committed it to paper. I knew his pastry mix, the Bramley apples, the cinnamon, cloves, lemon and the egg white glaze. *King George's apple pie recipe was mine!*

One night, at around midnight I was feeling very hungry. All the guests were sleeping by now and there were no more trays to be delivered so, in clandestine fashion, I entered the hotel fridge, which was like a bank vault that you walked into, to help myself. My usual attire was a dinner suit but I was minus my jacket.

To my left were three large tray-racks and in the centre of one of them were, yes you've guessed it, two magnificent, untouched trays of apple pie. I began to salivate uncontrollably. I stood there greedily eating great slices of George's pie, and with sides of beef and pork hanging all around me, frozen, it was extremely cold. When I'd had my fill I tried the door to get out. Unfortunately, there was something faulty with the lock and it quickly dawned on me I was imprisoned. For some strange and unknown reason, the safety over-ride was broken too. It crossed my mind momentarily that George might have tampered with it. I was freezing just in shirtsleeves. I didn't know what to do. I called out, but the fridge walls were thick and there was no one around to hear me in any case. All the guests were tucked up in bed, deep in the arms of Morpheus and well away from the kitchen.

I began to shiver uncontrollably, and resorted to practise *karate* to keep warm.

Fay, the little Greek breakfast cook finally opened the fridge door, but only after I'd been in there for six-and-a-half-hours! The second chef's words, 'He'll have your guts for garters' reverberated in my mind. My appetite for apple pie diminished quite rapidly after that. It was sheer greed, and I got my comeuppance.

I was reminded of an old Buddhist proverb: *'Greed is like a viper hiding in a flower garden, it poisons all those who come in search of beauty'.*

Take Your Partners for a *Conger*

We were in Sydney, and decided to go snorkelling. Heading down to Rushcutters Bay, we discovered a little ill-kept road that opened onto a rocky area on the edge of Sydney Harbour. In our naivety, we thought the harbour was safe. We couldn't work out why we were the only ones there, and put it down to good luck, it being such a lovely spot and the water was crystal clear. We all three wasted no time, changed and put on our snorkelling gear. It was great fun chasing the fish around. We had one spear-gun between us, so only one person went into the water at a time to avoid an accident. It was my turn; Garry and Jeff were on the rocks, and down I went.

I'd swum competitively as a teenager and was able to hold my breath perhaps longer than most, having trained in the Japanese way of swimming breast stroke underwater. In the 1950s, Olympic size swimming pools were 50 metres long and for the 200 metres event in breast stroke, the Japanese realized you could swim faster underwater that on top. Consequently, in the 1956 Olympic games in Melbourne, Masaru Furukawa swam the 200 metres underwater and only came up at the three turns to take a breath. Clever—and not only did he win gold, he also broke the world and Olympic records as well.

So, I did a duck-dive and went down to the bottom of the harbour, which at that spot was about forty-feet deep. As you descend it's necessary to equalise the pressure in your ears. When I got to the bottom, there were all kinds of beautifully coloured fish—angelfish were everywhere, and I gazed upwards and could see the surface way up above; the rays of the sun penetrating downwards. I wasn't able to stay down very long of course, and started to think about swimming back up, knowing full well that I'd have to equalize the pressure on the way to the surface.

I was about to begin my ascent, swimming past some large rocks when suddenly, coming straight at me out of a crack in those rocks, was a truly massive conger eel—our heads were on a collision course—and as it approached it opened its enormous jaws.

This creature's mouth wasn't normal; it was disproportionate to its body, and I looked through my mask right into a mouth which I estimated at the time could engulf my head. Aiming the spear gun I pulled the trigger. The bolt missed the creature entirely and sped on harmlessly.

I turned back on myself and kicked it in the mouth with my flippers as it came for me. I was panicking and trying to swim upwards at the same time, with little breath left in my lungs. There were bubbles everywhere, and I couldn't see the eel as I thrashed about, terrified it was going to bite me on my blind side, wherever that might be.

A Large Conger Eel

Eventually, I got to the surface. "Garry! Jeff!" I screamed, "Get me out! Get me out!" I was in a state of absolute panic, and as they struggled to pull me ashore, I cut my hands, legs and feet on the razor-sharp rocks. Having come face-to-face with that damn thing, I never, ever, went into Sydney Harbour again.

I later read, however, that there had only been four fatal attacks there since 1937, and they had all been from sharks. I thought, 'That may be so, but I'm not risking it again.' I now know why the public are always being alerted to the dangers of those waters by the authorities, and why no one swims at Rushcutters Bay—*apart from the crazy British.*

...and all because the lady loves

Milk Tray

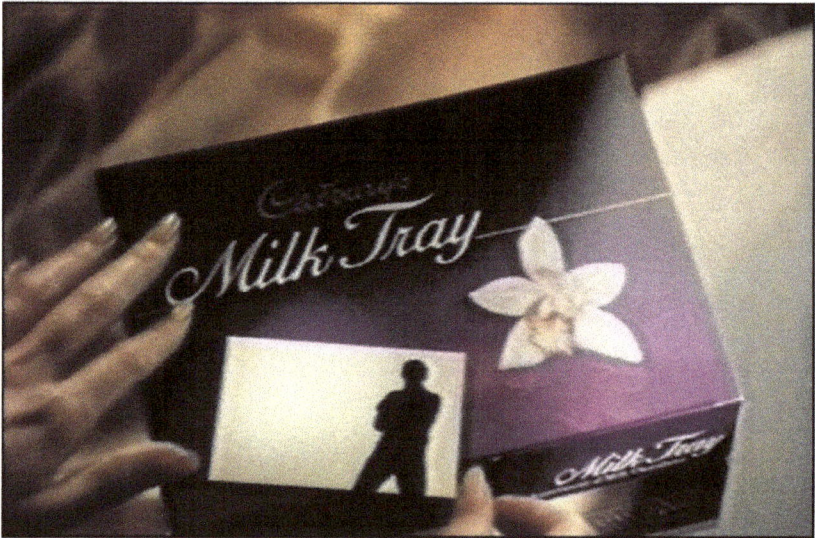

In 1968 to 2003, Cadbury's chocolate was advertised by 'The Milk Tray Man', a tough James Bond style figure who undertook daunting raids to surreptitiously deliver a box of Milk Tray chocolates to a lady. There were nineteen adverts in the series and six actors played the Milk Tray Man. Gary Myers, who is the most recognisable as the action hero, starred in eleven of them between 1968 and 1987. In the TV advertisements, he battled sharks, raging torrents and avalanches etc. to bring his lady a box of Cadbury's Milk Tray.

Gary Myers, a former Australian soldier, was chosen for his chiselled looks and resemblance to Bond supremo Sean Connery. Interestingly, Myers shared the same theatrical agent as fellow

Australian George Lazenby, who played 007 in *On Her Majesty's Secret Service*. Although Lazenby never played the Milk Tray Man himself, many assume he actually did. The movie was filmed in Switzerland, the spiritual home of milk chocolate and those Swiss locations would have allowed Lazenby to demonstrate his prowess on skis, just like the Milk Tray Man in the avalanche and cable car adverts.

Any man today performing acts of derring-do while dressed in black, especially where chocolates are involved, is soon dubbed a Milk Tray Man.

Twenty-years after leaving Australia, I went back with my wife in 1986 for a holiday. We landed in Perth and after spending a week there, headed for Alice Springs. I had organised a trip into the outback with an Aboriginal guide. Sleeping under canvas and the stars was quite incredible, then it was on to Adelaide with its countless memories from so long ago.

I hired a car and we drove south and onto the Great Ocean Road to Melbourne. After a few days we headed north, and spent some time in Canberra before reaching Sydney. We had decided to stay in Cronulla but eventually ended up at Bondi Beach, where we rented an apartment on Campbell Parade. The sea was too rough for swimming so we made our way to the next bay at Tamarama beach. It was beautiful, very hot and sunny and I decided to walk up the beach and buy a couple of cold Cokes from the little kiosk at the top.

I ordered them from the man behind the counter and as he returned I looked at him and said. "I know you—I really do know you." He half smiled and looked down. When he finally looked up he was smiling broadly. "You're him aren't you—you're the Milk Tray Man!" Gary Myers and I shook hands and had the most interesting conversation. My final question to Gary was this. "After 16 years as the best Milk Tray Man ever, why did you give up? You were absolutely superb." He smiled again, looked me straight in the eyes and simply said, John, "They found a younger man."

Gary Myers

"Wish Me Luck as You Wave Me Goodbye"

Sydney's Bondi Beach is not the nicest beach in the world, and I've heard recently that it has had problems with pollution, but it's huge, and there tends to be a lot of people there, especially during the surf carnivals and competitions. For many young men, to become a lifeguard on Bondi Beach is the ultimate accolade. One day, my brothers and I went down to the beach. The surf was up due to the offshore breeze, and the waves were building fast.

Novice board-riders didn't go out when conditions were like that, and although we weren't that bad at surfing, we shouldn't really have contemplated it. Surfing under those conditions can be very dangerous. Jeff didn't want to know, and Garry went out a little way, before returning. The swell was tremendous, with waves thirty-feet high. They rolled in as a set of seven, followed by a lull of about two minutes. I watched as men rode those big waves, and as impetuous as ever, thought that I'd like to have a go.

You just dream about this kind of wave if you're a board-rider, and the only other locations that generated waves like that in a well-known setting were in California and Hawaii. Anyway, there's a technique for getting out in such conditions, using your board, but I hadn't acquired the knack and had to wait for the lull in the sets and paddle like mad to get distance from the shore. I waxed my board and waited for the right moment. The seventh wave came, and off I went.

Now I had to get beyond the point where the first wave would break. I paddled like fury—one hundred metres, one hundred and fifty metres out. My arms were getting heavy and tired, and my neck was aching as I kept an eye on the water ahead. I could see the first wave beginning to pick up, gathering mass. I wasn't far enough out. I had to get to the point where the wave hadn't broken, because if it broke over me I'd be in serious trouble. I paddled as fast as I could, and gambled by putting all my strength into the action, but it soon became evident that I wasn't going to make it. I was scared— very, very scared.

There were no lifeguards out there, and by the time they'd have got to me it would have been too late. I let go of my board, tucked my chin on my chest, covered my ears, rolled up into a tight ball and took a deep breath. An enormous wall of water came crashing down on me. I lost all sense of direction. I was trying to swim upwards, but was swimming downwards instead. The sand went into my ears and nose, and the noise was deafening. I couldn't open my eyes. The water was pulverizing my lungs, but I had to keep the air in. It seemed like an eternity, but I managed to bob up and gasp for air. But I knew what was going to happen next, because that was the first of the seven waves and I was right in the firing line! I just had time to take a breath when the second one was on me.

It happened three times and although I virtually lived in the water as a youth, it was a nightmare experience. I finally got washed up on the beach coughing and spluttering, and the lifeguards came over to check me out. I never went out in such conditions again, and that experience taught me a lesson in life. It taught me only to gamble after I'd done my homework thoroughly. Unfortunately, I sometimes forgot it…

The Law of Karma:

Whatever you do in the world, good or bad—will always come back.

Since childhood, I'd had a fascination, an empathy I guess, with native North American Indians and Aborigines. Both were oppressed peoples, both had been abused and exploited by the white man (I remember, much later, reflecting on their similarities while standing on the rim of the Grand Canyon in America, looking down on the reservation of the Havasupi Tribe). I don't know why I was so interested in them; perhaps it had something to do with my upbringing.

Now that I was in the land of the Aborigine, I decided to investigate further. In Australia at the time, Aborigines were like the 'Blacks' now known as African Americans, of the southern states of America. They were poor, down-trodden, perceived as lacking academic ability, living in a 'world of dreams', with many of them having travelled to the cities, ending up as alcoholics. You could see them on the street corners in Sydney, drunk. They didn't do themselves any favours and they had a bad name amongst the whites. I gained the firm impression that Aborigines just couldn't make it in the white man's world—I don't know if it has changed very much since.

I was interested in the artefacts of these peoples, the tools and the weapons, and I was absolutely fascinated by the boomerang. I'd bought boomerangs, and after training or going for a run on the beach, I'd spend a great deal of time trying to master the skill of throwing one so that it might come back to me. However much I tried though, I could never get one to return. I broke a lot because the authentic ones are made from hard, but brittle wood from the mulga acacia shrub, and when boomerangs hit a large stone, they'd shatter. I spent a small fortune on them, but no one seemed to know how to throw one, even the Aborigines in the city—perhaps they didn't *want* to show me.

One day, I was in the outback in the north of South Australia with Joan, when we visited an Aborigine settlement. White people normally kept well out of these places. You had to respect the Aborigines' privacy, and they didn't really like uninvited white people coming there. My intention was to go and see these people, talk to them, and just be with them. We arrived at the settlement, where I saw an old man carving a boomerang about two feet across with a knife. We stopped the car, got out, said 'hello', and were invited to sit down. He offered us a drink and some damper, (unleavened bread), which is part of their staple diet, that had been baked in wood ash in the communal clay oven. In this way we got chatting.

I reckoned he must have been about seventy, but later he told me he was thirty-five. I was absolutely amazed, because he looked so haggard, but that's what life out in the Australian sun can do to you. As we were talking about boomerangs, I asked him if I could buy the one he was carving.

He said that traders from the city would come up and buy his stock. They paid him the proverbial 'peanuts' of course, so I gave him a reasonable price for it and the others that he'd made, and he was very happy.

It was a real education watching that man work, because with boomerangs it's all about aerodynamics—getting the lift from one edge. It really is very scientific.

I asked him to show me how to throw one, because we were sitting in a large open space. He said, "Don't move," and threw it. The boomerang went out, came back, went past us, turned again, and he caught it in the palms of his hands after it had completed a figure of eight, around us, standing in the middle. "Wow! How did you do that?" I asked, excitedly. His reply was that it was easy, and he beckoned me to have a go. I did, and it didn't come back, as usual. Then I tried again, and again. I asked him what I was doing wrong, because I knew there was a secret. He said, "Look. First of

110

all you are throwing straight ahead, and that's no good. You have to throw it into the wind at a forty-five degree angle of attack. Secondly, the secret is in the wrist, and he showed me the way to do it.

It reminded me of the wrist action in the *shuto-uchi* (knifehand-strike) before the *mae-geri* (front-kick) in *Heian Yondan*. So, I felt that the more I practised throwing the boomerang, the better my *shuto* would become. It was a case of killing two birds with one boomerang!

I threw the boomerang again, and to my absolute amazement, it landed at my feet after completing the figure-of-eight. The Aborigine picked it up, twisted it a little, and carved a thin sliver of wood from it. He knew exactly what to do. He took it as something of an honour that we'd taken an interest in him, but the honour was all ours. As we drove away, I felt a strange anxiety, and a desire to do *something* to help.

After we left Sydney, we went north into Queensland, then back into South Australia, returning to Adelaide via the Flinders Ranges. In the two years or so we were in Australia, we covered at least fifty-thousand miles.

Jeff and I trained in karate, where and when we could together. As soon as we got back to Adelaide I went straight to see Joan. I'd missed her terribly. Two days later Jeff and I went back to Moss Hollis's *dojo*.

We'd been away two months, and stayed in Adelaide until 20th August 1966, before returning home. Just before leaving Australia, after one and a half years of training, as I've already said, up to three hours a day, seven days a week, I was awarded my black belt by Moss. Jeff was awarded his brown belt.

My Time in OZ

by Jeff van Weenen

I was a baby boomer, born of English parents with bloodlines stretching across Europe. One of five children who grew up in the post-war suburbs of North London. I had a Secondary Modern education before starting work in a number of dead-end jobs. Living in Enfield, the only playgrounds were the remaining bombsites. Entertainment was non-existent and by hanging out with the wrong crowd, I saw myself drifting into a life of petty crime.

The late fifties were a very grey time. Smog before the smokeless zones, dull youth clubs, so it would surely only be a matter of time before I got my 'collar felt' by the law. One day, John came home with a copy of the *Daily Mail* and there was an advert for Australia and people wishing to go there for two years with skills the country needed. He asked Garry if he wanted to go, and he said "yes," as he was 'chomping-at-the-bit' to go somewhere—anywhere. I felt a bit left out, so I asked my dad if I could go too and he said "yes." We all had our medicals and interviews and waited for the results, which came very soon after, so we were on our way. I was only seventeen years old at the time but felt I was in for a great two years.

After a few months in Adelaide and an extremely bad experience, John and I joined a Karate club. It wasn't Garry's 'cup of tea' so he didn't come with us. There were a lot of people there all wearing karate suits and all had different coloured tags sewn onto their white belts. Some were hitting punch-bags whilst others were preforming strange moves. The black belt instructor introduced himself as Moss Hollis from England.

We joined immediately and over the next few months trained very hard. Eventually we both took our green belt examination and fortunately passed.

Maybe they based the character 'Rambo' on me!

About this time I managed to get a job at the John Martin's department store in the city. It only paid $75 a week—but it was work. Within weeks I had moved on and became a telegram boy in the Adelaide suburb of Hindmarsh. I kept the job until December when we left our apartment in Henley Beach and moved to the small seaside town of Semaphore.

I noticed an advertisement in the local paper—a company looking for grape pickers. It was a seasonal job up on the Murray River about a hundred miles east of Adelaide and was for three months with full board and good pay. So saying goodbye to the boys, I set off for a town called Monash. I spent fifteen hours on the train only to find I was the only one on it. Later I was told I had gotten on the slow train which was transporting horses and cows.

When I started work it was with a team of Italians and Greeks and the daily temperature was 43 degrees Centigrade. It was extremely hard work and to cap it all, I was staying with an old guy of eighty-five, an ex-picker, in a hut with spiders crawling up the walls. It was a really terrifying place but as I needed the money I had to stick it out.

At the end of a hard day there was nowhere to go. Everybody just slept, so I would go out into the yard and practise my karate moves. Well, one evening whilst training, a voice shouted out,

"Don't move, don't move." To my shock and horror there was a big snake right in front of me. I froze—the old man came over with a two-pronged stick, picked up the snake and flung it as far as he could. He told me later it was a brown snake and if it had bitten me, I would have been a 'gonna'—I knew then I had had a very lucky escape.

At night I would just lie in bed reading my karate book and watching the spiders going up and down the walls—very difficult to sleep I can tell you. The next day the old guy told me the one to watch out for was called a Huntsman spider. He said there is one of them living in a hole in the wall, behind the cooker and he feeds it every morning. It was then I decided to get the hell out of there. As luck would have it, John and Garry came to find me two days later—boy, was I happy. I threw my pot of grapes away, picked up my belongings and we drove away. Altogether, I saved one hundred dollars—big deal, but hey, we were on our way to Sydney.

Driving over the Sydney Harbour Bridge, wow, pretty spectacular but all we had heard of was Bondi Beach and when we saw it, it was like a dream come true. We found digs at Fletcher St in North Bondi and most days we were at the beach, then one day there was a commotion down at the water's edge. A baby shark had its grip on a little boy's leg and the lifeguard was trying to prise its mouth open to release it. Welcome to Bondi. I think there were shark-nets in place at that time but this baby got through.

It was pretty quiet at night, there wasn't much there for young people. The Rex Hotel where we used to have a counter lunch, a disco called the Thunderbird-a go-go (how very sixties), and one coffee bar. Not like it is today. Now we needed to get a job and all three of us started work at the Bronte Charles Hotel. My job was working at night in the cabaret bar picking glasses up off the tables and washing them up. One night there was a really big fight and I got pushed and my whole tray of glasses went over everyone at the table. People got cut quite badly, it was a real mess and guess what—I got the sack!

Earlier I had spoken to the drummer in the Terry King Showband. His name was Jerry, a really nice guy and he was Frank Sinatra's first call when he toured Australia. Jerry spoke to me one day and asked if I played drums as I was always watching him play. I said no and he then invited me to 'have a go'. Oddly, he seemed quite impressed with my impression of Ringo Starr and wanted me to stay in Sydney so he could tutor me. I apologised and told him we were going home soon to the old country but thanked him anyway. So that was that. You can't spend your life dwelling on what might have been…

Jeff on the way home, visiting Tahiti.

Soon after we had booked our return passage home and Garry's twentieth birthday, he got his 'call up' papers for Vietnam. He was informed he should report at a given address in Victoria for six weeks' training, before being shipped to Nam.

"F*** that," he said. "We've booked our passage home so let's get out of here"—and we did!

For what it's worth, I became a professional drummer in 1969 at Butlins Holiday Camp, backing up people like Matt Monroe, Diana Dors and Bert Weedon. Looking back, I have Jerry to thank and I'll always be grateful.

In retrospect, it was a great experience to go to Aussie in the early sixties. When I got home I saw my old mates, still down at the local pub and had many stories to tell them. A year later they all decided to go there themselves, to find out if I was telling the truth, and many never returned. It's a funny old world... But we three were the original trailblazers!

My Trip to Queensland

by Garry van Weenen

I had decided to go 'up north' before we returned to England and my destination was Queensland, setting my heart on reaching the fabulous 'Gold Coast'. I left the boys at Sydney's main railway station one chilly Monday afternoon. As the train pulled out, I experienced a mixture of emotions that I now know were perfectly normal for a twenty-year-old—apprehensive, scared that's for sure, but above all an overwhelming feeling of excitement.

I looked out of the carriage window and I could just see the boys, as arranged, waving their white handkerchiefs, I waved mine in reply and then they were gone. The train was quite full but I managed to get a seat by the window. They were comfortable, just as well for I would be sitting here for fifteen hours. The corridor outside the compartments enabled you to stretch your legs and walk the whole length of the train. I thought I'd explore.

Halfway down the corridor I came upon the restaurant car, so I ordered some tea and a slice of cake and sat down. The young lady opposite me was reading, a moment later she looked up and we both smiled. I introduced myself and she told me her name was Christine. She had come to Australia a month before us from England and was taking up a position as a nanny with an Australian family in Rockhamton, north of Brisbane where I was getting off.

She was so interested in our story and the problems we had faced since we arrived and as we sat there engrossed in conversation, I hardly noticed that I was becoming quite attached to her. Finally we parted company but not before promising to meet in the morning for breakfast. Sleeping was difficult sitting up, and lying down was not an option as most of the seats had been taken. It was an uncomfortable night to say the least and at 7.00am I made my way

117

to the restaurant car. I really didn't expect her to be there, but she was and smiled as I entered the carriage. An hour after breakfast the train pulled into Newcastle and, with a thirty-minute stay, we got off and had a cup of tea in the station café.

Then it was off again to Port Macquarie, Coffs Harbour and Grafton where we had another thirty-minute stop. Christine and I walked into the town lined with Jacaranda trees (Grafton is known as the city of Jacaranda) displaying a vivid purple coloured flower coupled with a unique aroma. We walked quickly back to the train, and just in time too. Soon we were heading for Brisbane and my destination that day. At the station, she followed me onto the platform. I kissed her on the cheek, held her lightly in my arms as we said our tearful goodbye.

We exchanged addresses and promised to write. As the train pulled away taking her with it, a sense of loss came over me. I remember shouting, "Please write." She smiled and shouted, "Yes." She never did and I'm sorry to say, neither did I, and I never saw her again.

I stayed in Brisbane that evening at the YMCA and in the morning, started on my way back to Sydney. I hitch-hiked all the way there and en-route met so many people. At Coolangatta, I was lent a surf-board and had an amazing time in the ocean. That night, I stayed at the surf club and slept on the floor. I wasn't alone, for there must have been about twenty surfers bedded down there, male and female, all sleeping, but full of anticipation for the dawn that would come bringing with it a decent swell.

As the first rays of the sun appeared over the ocean, they awoke, didn't speak, unzipped their sleeping bags and, picking up their boards and wax, ran to the sea. It was the first time I had witnessed an unspoken camaraderie between a group of young people. I couldn't help but feel a little cowardly as I closed my eyes and went back to sleep.

Garry king of the surf

119

Two hours later they were back and I joined them for breakfast at a little mobile 'pie' stall that had suddenly materialised from nowhere. With a delicious pie and hot coffee in my stomach, I bade farewell to everyone and headed for the highway once again. I was lucky in getting a lift so quickly and soon arrived back at Grafton, the city of the Jacaranda. I walked the same route that Christine and I had taken a short time before, and I looked forward to hearing from her.

I was very fortunate in getting some good rides and stayed in Coffs Harbour and Port Macquarie for the next two nights before setting out on the long stretch to Newcastle. I felt my luck was running out having waited for three hours by the roadside, that was until an old couple pulled up and very kindly gave me a lift all the way to Newcastle. They were absolutely wonderful and I really enjoyed their company. I was able to show my appreciation for what they had done by paying the bill when we stopped for a bite to eat—they were so grateful…

In Newcastle I cheated and caught the train back to Sydney, but I never let on to John and Jeff. When I arrived back, the boys were good and I told them all about my northern adventure. We went out and had a few beers and looked forward to seeing our family again.

A few days later a letter came for me from the Australian Government. It informed me that as I had reached my twentieth birthday, I was required to enlist for the military and in all probability now that Australia had entered the war with Vietnam, I would be called upon to undertake active service.

We sat down that evening and discussed the situation and were unanimous that I should not go. The following day we booked our passages to England on the Shaw Saville's *Northern Star*. I wrote to the government office informing them of my impending departure. I was informed that as I had already booked my passage to England I would be allowed to go but if for any reason I did not, I must inform the government immediately, and my selection for the Military would commence.

That was in July 1966 and the *Northern Star* was due to sail on 20th August from Melbourne. John kept in touch daily with Joan and her mother and they booked their passages to coincide with ours. They flew to Melbourne on 19th August as we did from Sydney where we rendezvoused at a Melbourne hotel. The next day we sailed on the long voyage to England.

Grafton, New South Wales, the city of the Jacaranda.
Soooo Beautiful.

The Long Journey Home

We left Melbourne to return to England aboard the thirty-thousand ton SS *Northern Star* of the Shaw Saville Line. The trip was to take six weeks. I was not a good sea traveller, but I had no option, because we didn't have the funds to fly back.

Although I had built myself a good life in Australia, I missed England terribly. It may sound trite, but I missed things like the Tower of London and Buckingham Palace. I missed what I'd been brought up with, and England's history. I liked what England stood for and I've always been very patriotic.

I don't know why I feel this way; I certainly didn't get it from my father. Australia doesn't really have that much of a heritage; it's all relatively new in comparison. I went to the Captain Cook sites and similar attractions, but it just wasn't the same and I missed the Old Country.

I had a longing to come home, and I wasn't alone, for Joan's mother was missing England too. Joan and Hilda joined us on the trip back. Joan's brother Tony stayed on, made a life for himself before returning to England some years later in the seventies. He married Barbara, had a daughter Nicola and adopted Barbara's son Lee. In 1984, Tony moved back to Australia with his family. Tony passed away after a two-year illness from Asbestosis in 2011.

I was happy that I wasn't to be parted from Joan. The first port of call was Sydney and then we crossed the Tasman Sea to Auckland. When we did stop and had a few days on land, it was an enormous relief for me to get off the ship. On New Zealand's North Island, we went to see the geysers at Rotorua, which were spectacular, then on to Wellington.

With two days at leisure in the capital, Joan and her mother decided to go on a shopping spree, whilst Garry, Jeff and I thought it a great opportunity to explore the North Island.

Hiring a four-wheel drive off-road vehicle, we set off early one morning heading for the mountain range south of Lake Taupo in the island's centre. The further inland we drove, after passing Palmerston North, it was noticeable how sparsely populated it became.

I had seen photographs of Milford Sound on New Zealand's South Island and like most, had marvelled at its natural beauty, but what we were seeing now was simply stunning. With rugged mountains rising steeply to the left, and a sheer drop into a ravine on the right, it seemed an ideal spot to pull over and explore. It was so peaceful—you could have heard a pin drop.

Through a gap in the pine trees, a fast flowing river at the bottom of the ravine was visible. It curled like a giant snake, a greenish blue, through what appeared to be a canyon. Little needed to be said, each knew what the other was thinking—we were going down!

We estimated it would take at least an hour. In reality it took two before we found ourselves by the riverbank. The canyon, which was no more than four-hundred-metres long, lay downstream to our right. Unanimously, we agreed to walk upstream, following the bank. The terrain was flat and we made good progress. It was absolutely beautiful, as if we were the only humans on earth. I estimated the river was about thirty metres across. Crouching down, I put my hand into the water. It was crystal clear, and cold!

We had gone about a mile. The scent of the pine trees filled our nostrils and beneath our feet, a carpet of wild flowers shimmered in the intermittent sunshine. I looked at my watch—it was midday. The sun's rays had barely penetrated this deep crevasse, but this was as light as it was going to get. It was time to think about returning to our car, which could take anything up to three hours.

Suddenly we heard an eerie sound coming from the forest. "What the hell was that?" asked Jeff. "God knows," said Garry, "but let's get out of here." Before we could turn to go, a huge animal appeared out of the trees. At first I thought it was a pig; seconds later I *knew* it was a wild boar—he couldn't take his eyes off us, we had disturbed him and he looked *mean*. Unfortunately for us, it was lunch-time—his!

"Let's get out of here," I shouted, as we turned and ran back whence we came. I glanced behind and it appeared the creature was gaining on us. Now we were in the open with the river on our left. Panic stricken, I looked in vain for anything that could be used as a weapon—there was nothing. We all knew the river might be our only option, no matter how uninviting. The water seemed to have stopped flowing, and then it dawned on me we were probably running at the same speed. I was aware of a 'thumping'; was it the black boar, or was it my heart? It turned out to be both!

I could almost feel its hot breath on my back. I shouted to Garry and Jeff to jump, and they leaped into mid-air. In the confusion I lost my footing, tripped, and fell headfirst into the river. For some unknown reason we didn't feel the cold but were aware of the fast-flowing current. As I bobbed up, I could see the black boar just standing there, receding into the distance. Fortunately for us, there appeared to be a sandbank up ahead and we were able to wade ashore. Surprisingly, the river was not very deep and its bed was covered with large white pebbles.

It had been an amazing experience. We took off our clothes, wrung them out, before dressing and retracing our footsteps along the bank. Finally, the long and arduous climb up the mountain to our car. By the time we reached it the light was fading fast, but our clothing had dried out completely. If the truth was known, we were thoroughly exhausted.

Three hours later found us back in Wellington. The *Northern Star*, berthed in the harbour, could be seen from a distance and we drove in her direction.

Three extremely tired and dishevelled passengers climbed the gangplank, went straight to their cabin and collapsed. After failing to appear at dinner, Joan came looking for us. "What's that strange smell?" she enquired. "What smell?" I groaned. "Where on earth have you three been to?" she asked.

Not waiting for a reply and pinching her nose, she turned, switched out the light and quietly closed the door behind her. By that time, we were fast asleep once more.

Sailing out of the capital, my brothers and I took up a position at the bow of the liner. There was a storm approaching and enormous waves from the Southern Ocean were rushing in to greet us.

Just the thought that we were heading out into that made us feel ill. The first wave hit, flooding the deck, and we realised what we were in for. By the time I'd got below on F Deck, just after leaving Wellington Harbour, I was feeling really ill and I was sick in the corridor before I'd even reached my cabin. For the next week, until we berthed off Rarotonga, one of the Cook Islands in the Pacific, I was laid up with sea-sickness. I didn't eat anything, had only sips of water, which I immediately brought up. I just stayed in my bunk.

At Rarotonga, due to the shallow water, the natives would sail out and ferry passengers to the island in dug-outs. We had a lovely barbecue on the beach. I enjoyed our stay immensely.

Our next port of call was Tahiti in the Society Islands, French Polynesia. Approaching the luscious green island, we saw a majestic mountain range towering high above us, and I felt like a member of the crew aboard the *Bounty*, of mutiny fame in 1789, who went to the island to collect bread-fruit plants with a view to introducing them to the West Indies—remember, films inspired my travel!

I later learned that Captain Bligh had been appointed Governor of New South Wales (1806—interesting.) However, Papeete, the island's capital, was a real eye-opener. It was dirty, squalid, and a big disappointment. After Tahiti, we crossed the Equator to Mexico.

In Tahiti

126

Knocked Out by a Little Urchin

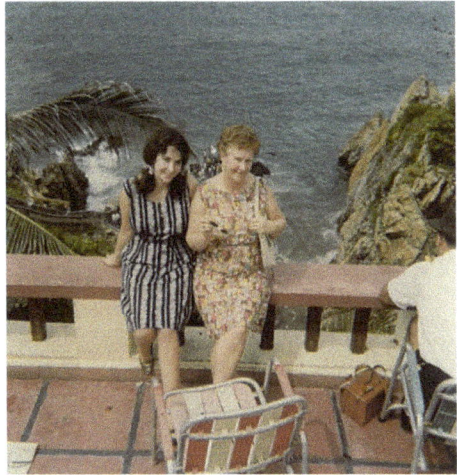

Joan and her mother relaxing in Acapulco in 1966.

Behind them is the place where Elvis Presley performed his high dive from the cliffs in the movie 'Fun in Acapulco' in 1963. His co-star was Ursula Andress.

During our brief respite in Acapulco, we naturally made the most of the beach. Garry, Jeff and I swam out about half a mile, but we were always looking down and around in that crystal clear water for sharks—mind you, I don't know what we would have done if any had come our way. Suddenly, below me, I saw something large and dark. A sickening shudder of fear went through me, an all-embracing shock and, instinctively, I kicked out violently, much as I had done with the conger eel. This dark object, much to my relief, was a jutting rock, part of a reef, but I'd come upon it unexpectedly and the light and movement of the water played tricks, making it seem alive.

Because my mind was focused on sharks, I saw what I was expecting to see. As I thrust out my leg, my foot struck the rock.

Now, as bad luck would have it, on the very spot I kicked was an enormous sea urchin, and the spines went deep into my foot. As I broke away, they snapped off and were left embedded. Unfortunately, those spines were poisonous, and it was necessary to have treatment otherwise I would have a real problem, and there

I was half a mile out in the Pacific Ocean. As I swam back, I could feel the poison taking effect, and by the time I got to the beach, I was delirious.

I was later told that my swimming style looked like a beginner's. My brothers had to help me out of the water, and I began to lose consciousness. All I remember was a large, muscular, black lifeguard, who picked me up and carried me back to his hut. He gave me some medicine, put a dressing on my foot, and it took about an hour for me to completely regain consciousness. All the black puncture marks were still visible on my foot, but the lifeguard applied some homemade medication that dissolved the spines.

Then we sailed south and through the Panama Canal into the Atlantic and docked at Curaçao, before crossing the Caribbean to Kingston, Jamaica. The ships in port were loading logwood, sugar, molasses, rum, bananas and many other products indigenous to the island. We disembarked and all had a great night out on the town.

Five days later, after a relatively uneventful Atlantic crossing, Lisbon's white buildings with their red-tiled roofs shimmering in the sun came into view. Our time ashore was enjoyable, but if the truth be known, we were all looking forward to seeing England once again, and our parents, family and friends. They say 'the last mile home is the longest', and those 48 hours it took *The Northern Star* to sail across the Bay of Biscay and into the English Channel passed agonizingly slowly. Finally, the great ocean liner steamed into Southampton Water, and we were home.

It was a strange feeling. Several thousand people lined the dock, all peering upwards, frantically scanning the main decks for their friends and loved ones—as we in turn looked down. Eventually, Garry spotted our parents with brother Derek and sister Linda, and within an hour, we were reunited with them. Joan and her mother, although a trifle apprehensive about meeting the family, were welcomed with open arms. Now it was time to get on with our lives. What I didn't know was that as one door was closing, another was about to open—a door through which Destiny had ordained I pass.

Joan and Hilda returned to Manchester and most weekends I commuted the two hundred miles to see them. I went back to work in the motor trade, with my friend, Mick Harton who had a car showrooms in Enfield. My job was to clean cars and motorbikes, with the occasional bit of mechanical work, but I was chiefly involved in preparing cars and bikes for sale. I had actually worked for Mick before I left for Australia. Strange as it might seem, after all my adventures, I didn't feel disappointed about coming back to the same job, because Mick and I got on really well together, so much so that he invited me to become his partner in the business. I accepted but was a little shell-shocked at his generosity. In the following three weeks I worked very hard and stayed on most evenings preparing vehicles for sale and I wanted to show him how grateful I was for the confidence he had in me. Then, on a Saturday morning, he told me the good news. "In the past three weeks John, we have made a staggering £1000 profit, come on," he said, "let's go and enjoy a little retail therapy, you certainly deserve it." With that he gave me £500!

My wardrobe was virtually non-existent and as we walked into Enfield Town and headed for the shops, I could feel the comforting bulge in my pocket of all that money.

Suddenly, Mick stopped walking. I could see he was sweating profusely and was trying to loosen his tie. I caught him as he collapsed on the pavement, unconscious. The whole left-hand side of his face and neck had turned a dark blue. Someone called an ambulance and minutes later we were heading for North Middlesex Hospital in Edmonton where doctors saw him immediately. That afternoon he was transferred to the intensive care unit and I was allowed to stay with him. I did so all that day and night, after having been told he had had a cerebral haemorrhage. During the night I could think of nothing but his generosity, the business and my older friend, who although twenty years my senior was just forty-five years old.

At 9.30am, on that Autumn Sunday morning in early October, Mick Harton died.

Anyone For a Starter?

Naturally, we were glad to be back home and after a couple of months decided to have a reunion party and invite all our old friends. It was tactfully suggested to our parents that a nice weekend away at our expense was just what they needed. My father was suspicious of his sons' newfound generosity, but was persuaded to go.

The party was a great success and went on throughout Saturday night and Sunday morning. At around 5.00am, Jeff and I decided to get a little fresh air and went for a stroll. It was a cold autumnal morning and nothing stirred. We stood talking at the crossroads at Baker Street. Enfield Town was a mile or so away to our left, Forty Hill half that distance to our right, and it was from the latter direction that trouble came.

In the still morning air, we heard a car coming towards us some time before we saw it. We took no notice, other than to remark that other folk were up at this hour too. The car slowed down and stopped about five yards from us. In the vehicle were three unsavoury looking characters, whom I deemed to be in their thirties. All the men got out and went to the boot. Jeff and I naturally assumed that they'd broken down and carried on talking. I remember thinking that if they needed any assistance I might well be able to help.

One man appeared from behind the car carrying a 'starter motor', and as he walked to the front of the car, nearest us, I could see that he was holding the motor by the shaft and Bendix. The car's bonnet was down and something told me that things weren't quite right. When he reached the front of the car, he carried on walking, and before I knew what was happening, he'd swung the starter motor in a wide arc over his head with the intention of bringing it down on my skull! Hindsight is a wonderful thing, for side-stepping with an immediate counter would have been the perfect response. However, the technique didn't occur to me at that moment, and as the motor came down on me, I reacted with a full *age-uke* (upper-rising-block). It was an instinctive act; and I'd learned the block on day one of my karate training.

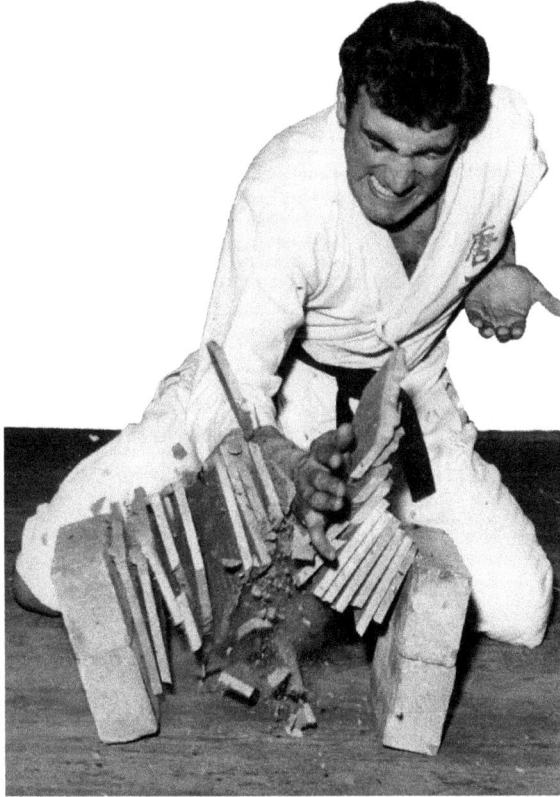

A demonstration of tile breaking for the opening of The Enfield School of Karate in December 1966.

An *upper rising block* may be a good technique for blocking a straight punch to the head, but it is not the ideal choice for blocking a starter motor being brought down onto your skull with great force. My timing and focus were immaculate, but the shock on the blocking arm was devastating; how it didn't break is a mystery to this day.

131

The block had taken most of the force and sufficiently jarred my opponent's arm so that he dropped the starter motor, but the momentum of the swing and his letting go, ensured that it fell on my head. I crashed to the pavement. I wasn't unconscious, but I was pretty close to it.

As luck would have it, before this lunatic and his mates could set upon Jeff and finish me off, out of the silence of that early morning, around the corner came some of our guests, returning home, and the men sped off. The pain was excruciating, and I was taken to Chase Farm Hospital and required eight stitches. Although I was injured, I can say with all honesty that karate saved my life that day. I have absolutely no idea why I was set upon. It was just mindless violence of an *extreme* kind.

Masutatsu Oyama

I n Australia, I had been a great fan of karate Master Masutatsu Oyama and actually wrote to him when we got back home (10th February 1967). I had read his books; found them both captivating and dynamic, and he seemed to me to be much larger than life. I desperately wanted to train with him, and wrote asking whether this would be possible. The following letter has not been grammatically corrected:

"Dear Mr. Weenen,

I have received your letter of 10th February. I am sorry that I have not written to you soon. Because I am very busy. I am glad to hear that you would like to come and study karate at my dojo. But the practicing in Japan is very hard. You cannot imagine. It is so hard that several students stopped training and [never?] came back. I am sorry to say but it is very difficult to find a job. There are several insurance companies in Japan. If you work there it is easy to come. Otherwise it is very difficult. It takes £40 a month for living and £2 10s a month (entrance fee is £5). If you learn the real meaning of karate I will be very glad. Mr. J. Jarvis came to my dojo from England and he will stay for one year. Two students came from Holland. One came from Spain. They do not work and are only practising. I am sorry but I cannot help you financially.

Sincerely Yours, Masutatsu Oyama"

To my utter delight, I actually got a reply (letter dated 21st March 1967), and Oyama cordially invited me to train at his *dojo*. Well, as you can imagine, this was like a dream, and I just had to go to Tokyo.

During the first few months of the New Year 1967 I planned the trip, and was arranging to leave in August. Jeff couldn't go because he didn't have the money, and was going to keep the *dojo* running in my absence. I made enquiries at the Japanese Embassy, but was told that unless I had a job to go to a visa wouldn't be granted. I tried to arrange employment in Tokyo, but it was impossible, and I was very disheartened for a while.

Finally I decided to take a chance and just go. If there was a way into Japan, I would find it and in the meantime, I could get as far as the docks at Yokohama, after that, it was all in the lap of the gods.

Karate was just taking me over. Joan and I had intended getting married once we'd returned to England, and although I loved her dearly, the distance between us geographically was putting a strain on our relationship. To some extent we both began making our own lives. We took it in turn to visit each other on alternate weekends and then one Saturday at her home in Fallowfield, I told her of my desire to fulfil an ambition to go to Japan and train in Kyokushinkai karate. I informed her that in all probability I'd be away for six months or so and when I came back *I would be thoroughly qualified, have a career, be able to support her, and we would be comfortable financially and could get married.*

It was hard telling her the news; she was very upset. I knew that if I didn't go I'd always regret it, always resent it, and I couldn't live like that. I was twenty-six years old, had no skills or career and was desperately crying out for direction. I had never felt so strongly about anything before and my gut told me this was a chance and an opportunity I would be foolish not to take. Joan and I resolved to make the best of things however, and to write weekly, which we did. Six months was not an eternity and would pass quickly.

Joan and I maintained regular correspondence, but one fateful January morning in 1968, I opened a fragile blue airmail letter—it held terrible news for me. Joan's first boyfriend had proposed to her and they were making plans for a June wedding. She explained that she couldn't take the loneliness after my departure, that her old boyfriend had entered her life again just at the right moment, and that she realised she still loved him. I wrote back immediately, asking her to reconsider. I couldn't stand the thought of losing her after all we had been through.

Perhaps I'd taken her for granted, and as impulsive as ever, I didn't wait for a reply.

If only she had waited for me to come home, the things I had promised her would have come to fruition. *This photograph from the future* (see page 137) shows how important it was for me to go to Japan for a limited period and study the virtually unknown martial art of Karate. My intention was always to give her the best life possible. Who can say how different everything would have been for us both had her patience not run out.

Master Masutatsu Oyama 10th Dan

At a Buddhist Temple at Kamakura

A glimpse into the future

Farewell to the Japan Karate Association

By this time, I had sufficient funds from my English teaching to enable me to catch a plane from Haneda Airport to Hawaii, where, it so happened, the world surfing championships were being held on Sunset Beach. My two friends Eddie and Mick tried to persuade me to stay in Tokyo, but my mind was made up. Together with my student Harumi, they came to wave me off.

All three were in a very sober mood. I believe Eddie was very disillusioned by this time at the standards and ethics at the JKA; Mick was a pretty introverted type, and I didn't really know what he was thinking. Harumi didn't want me to go either, so it was a sad occasion leaving them all. I'd been showered with so many presents by my one hundred and fourteen English language students—cloth calendars, scrolls, fans, a kimono, a *sake* set, a pair of *geta*, a *kara-kasa,* (bamboo umbrella) and so on, they were extremely generous—I was very fortunate to have known such people.

I was quite content to leave Japan, albeit rather abruptly. Although I'd trained a lot at the JKA, I had never really looked forward to the lessons. There was always an overwhelming feeling of fear every time you stepped into the *dojo*. Once inside you couldn't leave and you had to train under whoever stood in front of the class. None of the instructors spoke English, so learning was not the easiest thing in the world.

As I once remarked, some of the JKA instructors at that time were still fighting the Pacific war. Seeing tall Westerners, those whom they had lost the war to, in their class wanting to know how to fight, was just too much for them to take. *It was also too much for me.*

Joan was the most important thing in my life and it looked like I was close to losing her. I had to speak with her face to face. I also wanted to get back to my club too. I just yearned to get on with my life. I felt that having been to Japan, seen what I'd seen—some of which I liked, some of which I didn't—I'd just had enough.

Yet a final glimpse into the future and the title of the H.G. Wells novel *Of Things To Come* springs to mind.

Although twenty-two years had passed since I left Japan, the spirit of Gichin Funakoshi the father of modern-day karate lived on.

Here in 1990, 1000 of my karate students came together after having raised £158,000 for cancer research. Prof. Norman Williams accepted the donation on behalf of The London Immuno-therapy Cancer Trust.

3000 miles—Los Angeles to New York on $11

A journey of 3,000 miles begins with the first step...

A few days later, whilst on another flight to Los Angeles, my money ran out. Emerging from the airport, I had eleven dollars in my pocket, and that was all. Master Hidetaka Nishiyama was based in California, but I didn't go to his *dojo*. I was too worried about Joan and how I was going to get home, and with those concerns constantly at the back of my mind, I didn't have the right mentality to train. I knew that if I could get to New York and telephone my old bank manager, a friend in Enfield, he would send me the fare, which was seventy-five pounds, to fly home. It would have cost twice as much to fly from Los Angeles to London, and I simply hadn't got the money so I had no choice whatsoever—the only way was to hitchhike to the East Coast. I stood outside Los Angeles airport wearing a thin blue anorak, looking in all directions, thinking, 'I've got to get across America, some three thousand miles. Which way shall I go?'

You may recall Mick Harton my friend who died of a cerebral haemorrhage; well Mick's wife Irene, had parents who lived in California. She had said a couple of years before that if I was ever out that way I should look them up. It was a long shot, but I thought it worth a try. I had a number, so I rang it and I got through to Jim and Dorothy Boddington, Irene's mum and dad, who lived in Wilmington, just twenty-two miles outside the city.

I was invited to call on them, and thought to myself, 'Thank God for that!' After several bus journeys, I finally arrived at

Wilmington. I went to the Post Office for directions, where a member of the staff knew Jim, so she telephoned him, and he said he'd come and pick me up. By this time I was down to about four dollars, and I must have looked a sorry sight standing there with my carrier bag, which housed my karate suit and little else.

Shortly afterwards, a Buick Wildcat, an enormous limousine, drove up, and Jim took me back to the family home in West Anaheim Drive, where I was made very, very welcome.

They wanted to hear all about my time in Japan and when I told them I intended hitch-hiking across the United States, they were horrified. They said I shouldn't do it as hitch-hiking wasn't allowed on the freeways, and that I'd have to go on the minor roads. I stayed with them for some time and they took me to all sorts of places. Beverley Hills was ostentatious—the wealth, the excess. Everything was 'over the top'. It was all a trifle superficial, but I reasoned, 'I'm here, so enter into the spirit.'

141

Disneyland was an engaging trip back into childhood. Santa Monica, Santa Barbara and San Diego were all enjoyable. I went to some of the film sets in Hollywood. I visited MGM—it's an unreal world—Tinsel Town indeed. People look for stars, but don't see them. When you haven't got money, as I hadn't, you're not part of it. Money is very important in America, more so than in Britain, where our class system operates on different values. Palos Verdes, where all the movie stars lived, had beautiful but ostentatious homes.

It didn't take the Boddingtons long to figure out that their guest was broke, and I offered to do any odd jobs they might need doing for my keep, because they were getting on in years. It was an ideal arrangement; I did the chores and they kept me in food and lodgings. After about a fortnight, I felt that it was time for me to move on, and they offered me five hundred dollars, a lot of money, over a beer. They were nice people and I refused to take it. Jim said that he didn't know of anyone who had hitch-hiked across America, and in the nicest possible way, tried to impress upon me what a huge undertaking it was. I recall him saying that it would be minus ten degrees centigrade in New York, and I was kitted out for the summer.

My pride was taking a beating; I felt both compromised and embarrassed, and said to Jim, "May I take one hundred dollars for an emergency?" I could get a Greyhound Bus across America for eighty-eight dollars, thinking that would cover me. I had no intention of keeping that money, and every intention of paying them back, which I did—within three months of arriving home.

Jim drove me to the bus station where I bought a ticket with the few dollars I had to Barstow. A few years before, I'd watched a television series called Route 66 (1960–63), where two young men, Buzz, played by George Maharis, and a his buddy Todd, in a Chevrolet Corvette Stingray, travelled Route 66, having adventures along the way. Unfortunately for me, that was a movie, a fantasy world, and as I was about to find out, a long way from reality.

However, I really liked that series, and from it I knew that Route 66 started at Barstow. I had, effectively, to hitch-hike five times the length of Britain so once there, I wasted no time. When the first few cars or trucks stopped, they asked me where I was going to, and when I said "New York," they thought I was mad, and drove off— without me. So I quickly realised that it was best to say the next town not too far away going east. Fortunately for me it worked. The sun was shining, and I got some good rides.

Joseph Maguire

Walking into the eastern Californian town of Needles in January 1968, I looked for a café where I could have breakfast. It was 8.30am and already the town was bustling with activity. It was a typical Western town, and many of the men I saw were coming to collect provisions, get their hair cut or pick up supplies for their ranch. After breakfast, I walked down the main road. It was a bright winter's morning yet there was real heat in

that Californian sun. The direction I was heading would bring colder weather and I knew by the time I reached New York it would be well below freezing.

I picked up a newspaper, and sat down outside a café that had a few tables and chairs in the sunshine.

I was sipping my coffee and found myself inadvertently staring at a man at the next table. He wore a Texan-style outfit, was probably in his sixties, and had long grey hair and long side-burns. "Howdy," he said, "I'm Joseph Maguire—what are you doing out here, boy?" I told him the story and he appeared quite enthralled.

His family lived in Los Angeles, and he had worked for a tobacco company, whilst he watched his two children grow into teenagers. Like so very many Americans he was part of the 'rat race', and after many years had reached the point in his life when he had had enough.

He built himself a shack in the middle of the Arizona desert and moved there. His wife would join him for a couple of weeks at a time, but it didn't work out… She hated the isolation as much as Joseph loved it, so they reached an amicable agreement whereby she would live in Los Angeles and he would live in his 'shack' in Arizona, and they would see each other occasionally.

Joseph was on his way to Arizona that morning, and invited me to travel with him and come and visit. It was the dustiest ride I'd had in my life, and it was early afternoon when we left Needles and drove eastwards. Six hours later after miles of nothing, crossing the state of Arizona, we arrived at an area known as Baldy Peak. It was in the foothills that Joseph had his shack.

That evening, we sat and had supper outside on the veranda. The view was one of splendid isolation, with no sign of man, or anything else man-made. It was beautiful, and only the buzz of the crickets and the croaking of frogs broke the incredible silence. The whole place had a very cleansing and calming effect on me, something I have rarely experienced since. It was easy to see why Joseph had gone to live there. His needs were few but he was fortunate in having saved for his retirement.

The nearest town was *fifty* miles away and he would drive there once a week to get provisions. A stream provided him with fresh water and his overheads were negligible. He had taken care of his wife financially and that was augmented by her own pension. After endless years in the 'rat race', Joseph Maguire had 'opted out'— and he loved it.

Much of his time was spent writing short stories and novels, which he hoped to get published by a friend in Phoenix. When he wasn't writing, he was reading. At that moment, he was halfway through *Doctrines of Buddhism.* I questioned him on *loneliness,* and he said it was not a word he was familiar with. He was content with his own company and without the distraction of people; he had time to think about life and its meaning.

In his own way he was quite remarkable and I've never met anyone of the same ilk. I stayed the night, and the following morning he drove me to the highway, where I could (hopefully) hitch a ride in an easterly direction. As we said our goodbyes, each knowing neither would see the other again, he slipped a small card into my hand. "If you follow what's written on that John-boy, you won't go far wrong." With that he was gone, his car obscured by the trail of dust as he turned onto the dirt road and headed back to his own very special 'Shangri-La'.

I stood there, motionless, watching the dust slowly moving across my field of vision, until I could just make out his red pickup truck in the distance, carving a path through the scrub. I felt sad, my eyes began to water—the bright morning sunshine was *obviously* having an effect. I looked at the card, it was a little 'misty', and as I screwed my eyes up in an attempt to clear my vision, a tear fell, bouncing onto the blue card before disappearing into the sand at my feet. It was entitled, 'My Philosophy', and read as follows:

'I do not choose to be a common man, it's my right to be uncommon if I can.
I seek opportunity—not security.
I do not wish to be a kept citizen, humbled, dulled, by having the state look after me,
I want to take the calculated risk, to dream and to build, to fail or succeed.

I refuse to barter incentive for the dole.
I prefer the challenges of life to the guaranteed existence, the thrill of fulfilment to the state calm of Utopia.
I will not trade freedom for beneficence, nor my dignity for a hand-out. I will never cower before any master, nor bend to any threat.
It is my heritage to stand erect, proud and unafraid; to think and act for myself and enjoy the benefits of my creation, and to face the world boldly and say—*this I have done.*'

Powerful stuff indeed! I looked up, there was no sign of him or his vehicle, only the lingering dust trail drifting slowly in the light breeze, and merging into the distant mist that hung gently on the mountain range beyond. Deep in thought, I began walking in an easterly direction, but lifts were few and far between and four-hours later, tired, I sat down by the roadside to rest.

A Ride to Nowhere

The next town was about fifty miles away. Eventually, a man picked me up on the edge of the freeway and we talked until it got dark as he drove into what seemed like the middle of nowhere. He stopped the car in the centre of the road and I enquired, "What's up?" He replied that he lived over there, and pointed to a track. In the distance, I could just make out the light of a dwelling about half a mile away. I got out, we said our goodbyes, and off he went down the dirt road. The only trouble was, I was stuck in the middle of the desert! I looked ahead and behind me—it was pitch black, I was cold and alone. The stars shone brightly in the heavens. Occasionally, a car would come along. I'd see a faint pinprick of light in the distance which, after several minutes, grew and split into two, but by the time the driver saw me he passed in that darkness. And who would pick up someone in the middle of the desert at night?

I didn't know what to do. I was freezing. Practising *kata* in that Sydney fridge seemed to have worked, so I went through the *Heian* in the middle of the road to keep warm, a few cars came, but none stopped. I didn't know how far it was to the next town, but I roughly knew how far it was back the way I'd come, so I started to walk. If a car's lights appeared going the other way, the way I really wanted to go, I'd walk across the road.

After quite some time, a car went past and the brake lights came on, followed by the reversing lights. A woman driver wound down the window and said, "Hi!" and I replied, "Good evening. Thank you for stopping." I explained what had happened. She knew from my accent that I was English. The woman introduced herself and said, "This is my daughter, Linda. Climb in." I wasn't sure what to make of this, but I was aware that her daughter was not unattractive, so I opened the rear door and got in, and we set off back towards the last town I had passed through.

Soon conversation flowed between us, and before we got into town the mother whispered, "I'm not taking you to town, you're coming home with us!" At that point, I was still feeling pretty cold, so was quite happy to go along with her suggestion. Within a short time the car had pulled up at their ranch. Both Linda and her mother Angie were very kind but, unfortunately, I had to move on and, reluctantly, bade my farewell after a couple of relaxing days.

There was a time whilst hitch-hiking when things became pretty desperate. I remembered, in the old hobo movies of the thirties and forties, how the tramps would jump on freight wagons on bends in the track when the trains slowed down. Thinking I'd have a go, one night I climbed onto a goods wagon like an American hobo. I didn't know where the train was going, only that it seemed to be heading north. My destination was east, but I didn't know what might come of it, and, exhausted, I drifted off to sleep aided by the movement of the train. A sudden jolt woke me as the train was entering a small town and jumping off before being discovered, my whereabouts a complete mystery, as I didn't have a map, I walked into town and found a cheap little guest-house where I could rest up.

Gus

Back on Route 66 I starting hitchhiking again and a gentleman by the name of Gus, a Kentucky farmer, picked me up. His station wagon was quite luxurious. He was driving home, a long journey, about eighteen hundred miles, and, because we 'got on like a house on fire', he offered to take me all the way. We shared the driving, which was nice for him. Because of weather problems, we went south, through Arizona and New Mexico, and into Texas and the town of El Paso, immortalized in song by the legendary Marty Robbins. We crossed the valley of the Rio Grande then on to Arkansas and Tennessee. I saw some incredible sights, including the town of Earp, the home of Wyatt Earp, and the Old Mission, famous in American history as the site of the Alamo.

Gus and I parted company at Nashville. I hadn't told him I had Jim's one hundred dollars, and when we got to Nashville he left me in the car and went off and bought me, unsolicited, a Greyhound Bus ticket to New York. He was a really nice guy and we were both sorry to say goodbye.

I've never thought of myself as being parsimonious but perhaps through guilt I've always wished I had mentioned to Gus about the $100 that Jim gave me.

Twenty-four hours later I was in New York lodging at a YMCA, and that YMCA was the worst place I've ever stayed in. Serious drug addicts were everywhere, and a menacing atmosphere hung over the place, so I decided to go out and walk the streets until nightfall, but the below zero temperatures meant that I was obliged to return to my dingy room—a tiny, frozen box in desperate need of a coat of paint. The goings-on outside my door in the insufficient light—the cursing, the fights—were scary. I just shut the door tight, got into bed with my clothes on, shivered myself into fitful bouts of sleep, and didn't come out again until the sun rose.

150

I left that YMCA in a hurry, and walked to the bank, sorted out my loan, and that afternoon flew back to Heathrow. I had been in America for three weeks. When I arrived home, I acquired a Wolseley 1500 car and without further ado went straight to Manchester to see Joan. We talked in a pub in the village of Withington. It was clear that she had made up her mind to marry her former boyfriend Peter Harney and it was a tearful occasion for both of us. We sobbed our hearts out. An hour later I left her at her front door, and never saw her again. The long drive back to Enfield was truly awful.

Coming to terms with the loss of Joan took a long time. What made matters worse was that I knew that she could have been mine if I hadn't gone to Japan; if I hadn't been so consumed with karate. In the months that followed I lost myself in training and karate took me over once again. Sometimes though, to this very day, I reflect on what might have been and in an instant those fifty-years and that vast distance melts away and I am back at Horseshoe Bay in South Australia with a beautiful young girl in  my arms whom I loved so very much. That memory will never fade, nor would I want it to, she was everything to me—*it was another time and another place.*

Epilogue

The Author's Life after OZ

D o I regret leaving Australia, after having spent just twenty-five months there, is a tantalising question which deserves an honest response? The answer is quite simply—no, and I'll tell you why.

Without a doubt, Australia is one of the best countries in the world in which to live. In my case I experienced it in the sixties as a migrant, then later as a tourist on three separate occasions in the seventies, eighties and nineties. However, living in a country is a totally different ball-game from holidaying there.

Regardless of which country you live in, there is one thing that influences your existence almost completely, you guessed it—money. As a migrant in Aussie during 1964/5, I had very little of the stuff and *no one wanted to know*. It was a harsh period and there were no state benefits available at all. You were on your own. Later, when I did quite well with an insurance company I worked for, doors began to open and when I gained my black belt in karate, people wanted to know me, showed me a little respect and became far more friendly. Actually, *I was still the same person*—just a touch more affluent!

When I returned to Australia on holiday in the decades that followed, I was financially comfortable and what an incredible difference that made. Everyone was nice. In taxis, restaurants, hotels and shops most treated me like a long lost brother. They were well practised in pretence, for they only wanted one thing from me—and as much of it as they could get. *I was still the same person,* but with slightly deeper pockets.

I've come to realise in life as I've got older that money is not the most important thing. Health, love, family and friendship are of far more value, but I have to concede, money does come in handy. I don't regret leaving Australia at all, as much as I loved it, purely because my life was meant to follow a different path that destiny had chosen for me.

Here's a story that will amuse you. In 1974, I read in a newspaper that Jaguar and Range Rover cars were in desperately short supply in Australia and were selling for double what they were in the UK. I had owned a Sahara Dust Range Rover for two years, more than the required fifteen months before you could import it into Australia. So with thoughts of becoming a big international motor dealer and making a nice profit, I despatched my gleaming vehicle to Melbourne. The journey would take six weeks. Firstly a boat from Ramsgate to Flushing in the Netherlands, then another cargo ship via China to Australia.

The plan was for me to fly to Melbourne and arrive two days before the ship, complete all necessary import regulations, collect my vehicle and drive to the nearest Range Rover dealer and sell it for a handsome profit. After a nightmare two days of going from department to department, I finally got the required paperwork and rushed to the car-pool office at the docks. It was there I learnt that the ship had been delayed for three days due to severe storms in the South China Sea. That was on Monday and it was suggested I should come back on Friday morning after the unloading. The real nightmare had begun.

At 9.00am on Friday I presented myself and was pointed in the direction of the main car park. Approaching it with understandable trepidation, the sight that greeted me sent shivers running down my spine. The car park was packed with 247 Range Rovers plus a smattering of Jaguars, and all had come off the one ship. *It was at this point I began to shed a tear.*

To cap it all, most were painted in Sahara Dust. Finding mine would not be easy and I could feel *a headache coming on.* Approaching my car, I instinctively knew something was wrong.

The driver's door had been hit and was badly damaged. The radio and stereo player had been ripped out of the dashboard, the rear window was broken, spare wheel gone and every conceivable accessory that I had placed in the car had been stolen. The engine wouldn't start due to a flat battery. *My headache was getting worse.*

A guy turned up with a pair of 'jump-leads', relieved me of ten dollars, and 'voila', the engine burst into life! Feeling a touch better, I moved the gear leaver into drive. Big mistake. A horrible crunching sound filled the cab before the engine stopped and all went quiet. The gearbox was broken and useless—my baby was going nowhere.

I shed a few more tears.

I made my way by taxi to the main Range Rover dealer in Melbourne. The manager came out to greet me and invited me into his office, I thought, what a nice man—I soon found out he wasn't. Together with a mechanic, he drove me to the dockyard in his shiny white Range Rover to inspect the damage which was worse than I thought. The engine had no oil pressure, the sump was split and the oil had gone. The gearbox was finished, smashed to bits as was the final drive—the list was endless.

"What's it worth to you?" I asked. "I'll give you five hundred dollars for scrap," he said.

"It would cost thousands to fly the parts out from British Leyland in Birmingham, it's just not worth it." I took the money, signed some documents and retreated back to my hotel and got inebriated. So much for my becoming a big international motor dealer. (Clever clogs.)

Before we parted company, the manager said he had seen it all before. The stevedores drive the cars off the Ramsgate cargo ship and play 'Dodgem cars' with the vehicles. Most get smashed, they think it's great fun. They do it at night and are gone by the morning. "If I were you," he said, "I should get on to the Ramsgate company as soon as possible—they must be insured I would have thought." I thanked him and said goodbye.

Whilst still at the docks before returning to my hotel, I listened with incredulity to two other tales of woe. An elderly man had approached me and began unsolicited to pour his heart out. His story was as equally lamentable as mine.

He had the same idea as me and had shipped out his shiny blue XJ6 Jaguar. As he stood on the dock, fate took a hand. One hundred feet above the wharf, the forward sling carrying his car snapped, and the vehicle slipped out of the remaining rear sling and plummeted headlong onto the concrete. The car concertinaed, yet remained nose down and vertical, with its boot wide open in the air. *The elderly gentleman needed sedation.*

The other story I heard that day at the Melbourne docks was from an affluent, well-to-do business man who had overheard my tale of woe. It concerned another Jaguar, this time a sports E Type. The prudent wealthy owner had despatched his beautiful 3.8 litre car to Australia in a container box and given explicit instructions that it should not be opened until he was present.

How the 1961 3.8 litre E-Type Jaguar looked prior to its demise.

After being parted from his 'pride and joy' for six long weeks, he presented himself accordingly for the official container opening. His friends were all present and the champagne was on ice.

What he didn't know was that a stevedore had opened the container before the boat sailed from Southampton and had *some fun.* He had obviously left the car *out of gear,* with the *handbrake off.* With hundreds of containers on board, all stacked up on one another, it was impossible for any crew member to hear anything untoward.

The glasses were filled and held high as the doors were ceremoniously opened. Nothing recognisable of the E-Type Jaguar remained. Most of it was on the floor—in pieces. During severe storms in the Southern Pacific, the car had been shunted backwards and forwards and from side to side, probably ten million times, before smashing itself to bits.

The Champagne had a distinctly acid taste...

Needless to say, after hearing those two stories, I high-tailed it out of Australia and headed back home to relative sanity.

Without doubt, I've had a very adventurous life but my stint of fifteen years working in the Balkans, running a charity delivering humanitarian aid has taken its toll. In all I undertook eighty-seven missions and was grateful to have a great team of volunteers who gave me the most amazing support throughout. Now after five years as the Albanian Consul here in Britain, my responsibilities have come to an end. However, even though I am getting on in years now, I still feel I've got one more project in me, and I know what I would like it to be.

In 2004, a documentary was made by the acclaimed journalist John Pilger in conjunction with Granada Television. It revealed how the United States conspired with Britain to forcibly expel Diego Garcia's indigenous people—the Chagossians—and deport them to slums in Mauritius and the Seychelles, where most live in dire poverty today. They were all British subjects and all 2000 of them were put onto a ship and eventually dumped in Port Lewis. After, the Chagossian's pet animals were all gassed by the Americans, the island was completely sanitised and a seventy-year lease given to them to build a military base there.

Many Chagossians who live in the UK just want to go home. They are old now and just want to be buried in the family graveyard on Diego Garcia. The seventy-year lease has just been renewed by the British Government and all the people of the Chagos Islands want is *a right of return. If they are given this in the near future, I would like to go with them and help in any way I can to rebuild their community.* As British subjects, they were treated abominably—our Government should be ashamed of itself—*I know I am.*

Just imagine if some officials knocked on your door tonight and told you England had been sold and you should pack one suitcase and report at Dover at 9.00am tomorrow morning for deportation—how would you feel? The tragedy is, we are all British citizens and even though the Chagossians were black, their rights should have been respected—and they weren't. An injustice has taken place here—we simply need to rectify it before it's too late, and they are all dead.

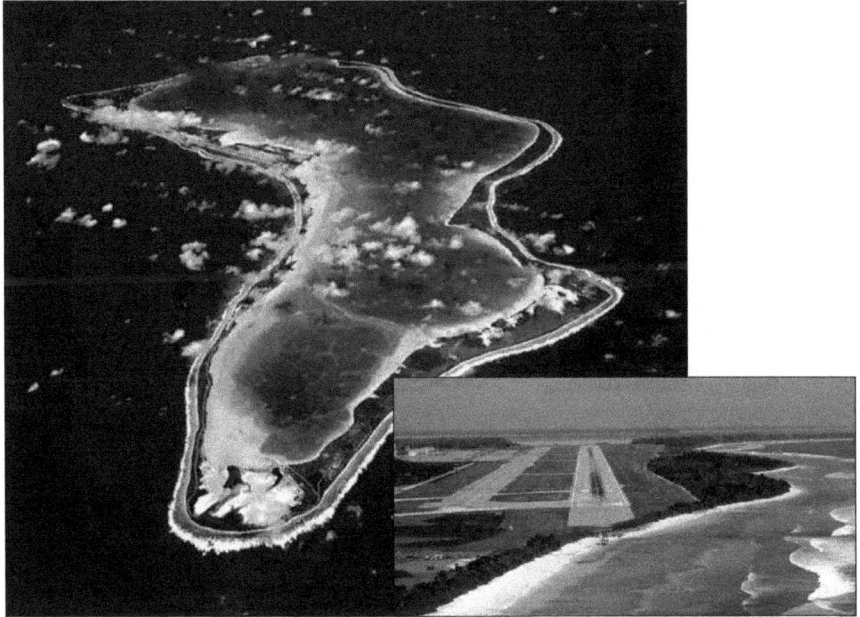

Diego Garcia, an atoll, the largest of the Chagos Islands lies in the middle of the Indian Ocean. Under the lease agreement with Britain, the Americans have built a runway over two miles long to accommodate their B-52 and Stealth Bombers and act as an emergency landing site for the space shuttle. The lagoon is a safe haven for American nuclear submarines. Despite all this power, fifty-years on, the American and British Governments still refuse to allow the now senior Chagossians to return home to die and be buried next to their parents and forebears.

John Pilger's documentary 'Stealing a Nation' is absolutely compelling viewing, as too is 'Diego Garcia-The Ugly History'. Both can be viewed on You Tube.

Joan's Life after OZ

Joan Derbyshire in Sidmouth, South Devon in June 2018

Finding Joan was not easy. The Internet flagged up 134 Joan Derbyshire's worldwide but eventually, I came across a photograph that was a possibility. However, the last time I had seen her she was only eighteen, now she would be seventy-years old.

Providence took a hand—*it was her.*

She had married her first love Peter Harney in June 1969. They had three sons and spent many happy years as the boys grew up. Eighteen-years later, in 1987, Joan and Peter decided to go their own separate ways and were divorced in 1988.

She threw herself into her job at St. Mary's Hospital, Manchester where she worked as a medical secretary. Sometime later in 1990, she met John Derbyshire. There was an immediate attraction, they fell in love and married in 1991. Joan's brother Tony, came from Australia especially to give her away.

In 2012, John and Joan decided to leave Manchester and start a new life together in Devon. They bought a house in the picturesque village of Newton Poppleford just outside Sidmouth and have been there ever since.

With the pending publication of *The Ten Pound Poms*, I thought it only right, as Joan was one of the main characters in the book, to allow her to read the manuscript before it went to press in case there was anything she disagreed with, or wanted to change. Together with my son Mansel I drove down to South Devon on 10th June 2018 and met the Derbyshires at 'Dukes' hotel in Sidmouth.

Needless to say, there was a certain amount of apprehension all round as Joan and I had not met each other for fifty years. It soon became apparent there was no need for concern for the conversation was extremely amicable and all that had been written was accurate with no changes being necessary.

Joan was happy to see me and meet my son Mansel for the first time and it was obvious a few skeletons had been laid to rest, bringing closure for all concerned. John Derbyshire is a lovely man and I was delighted they had found each other. I asked Joan if I could take a couple of photographs of her, "Of course," she said, without the slightest hesitation.

It was time to go. John and I shook hands and I felt there was a genuine understanding between us. Joan stepped towards me and we gave each other a hug—I kissed her on the cheek for the last time and our eyes held each other's momentarily. Then they both turned and walked away along the promenade and I watched them getting smaller and smaller, till they disappeared in the crowd. They never looked back—I thought for a moment they might, but neither needed to.

With mixed feelings of enormous joy for them both and a measure of misplaced melancholy, I crossed the road, met up with Mansel and walked towards the car to begin the long drive back home to Olney and Buckinghamshire. It was time to move on…

As we slipped onto the M5 Motorway just east of Exeter, an appropriate transcription of Robert Browning's words came to mind: *"One can never quite recapture, loves first fine careless rapture."*

'Home Thoughts From Abroad'

Jeff's Life after OZ

Returning to England in 1966, I noticed a significant cultural shift had taken place. Beatle-mania was still in full swing, and fresh political upheaval was rampant at Westminster. There were riots at the American Embassy, girls in micro skirts everywhere, and black and white TV had suddenly become a thing of the past being totally annihilated by colour. Things had changed in what seemed a short space of time, so now—it's back to a new reality.

I got a job at the local swimming pool for the summer and there I met Susan Sharman, who I was with for seven years.

My musical career began when my mother bought me my first drum-kit for forty-pounds, which was a considerable amount of money at that time, so I played along to The Rolling Stones' first album and probably annoyed the neighbours.

By that time, the British Blues Boom had begun, so Susan and I went along to see bands like Fleetwood Mac, Jimmy Hendrix, Taste, etc. Then of course the '67 summer of love (lol) was upon us, so we all became weekend hippies.

Around '68, Garry and I started a summer season as 'Redcoats' at Butlin's Holiday Camp at Skegness. Then in '69, I got my first real 'gig' as a professional drummer. In '72, I was recommended by a good friend of mine, Jed Ford, to join the well-known country band 'The Muskrats'. Fortunately, after an audition, they took me on, and I was with them for thirteen-years, playing all over England, Europe and even Alaska! When the band split-up, I joined 'The Poorboys', a great R&B band and stayed with them for ten-years.

In '95, I moved to France with my French girlfriend Cecile and now live in Paris. I work as a chauffeur for a limousine company driving tourists and celebrities around the city. It's an interesting job and over the past twenty years, I've met some really nice people, some of them movie stars and many from the world of show business. Surprisingly, none of them treated me badly. I guess I've been lucky. Cecile and I have two wonderful children, Joé who is sixteen and Amy who is twenty.

Le temps passe très vite—Time passes very quickly.

Jeff (centre) with 'The Muskrats' in 1981

Garry's Life after OZ

When I returned home from Australia, I had absolutely no idea what I was going to do for a career. Perhaps I still had thoughts of Bondi Beach circulating in my head, so I applied for a job as a lifeguard at the local outdoor swimming pool—and got it. The idea of working in the insurance field and wearing a collar and tie just didn't appeal to me at all.

In winter I was transferred to an indoor pool and it was here I became interested in teaching swimming. Fortunately, I passed all my exams with the Amateur Swimming Association (ASA) and this enabled me to secure a job at Butlins Holiday camps and Jeff came with me to work as a 'Redcoat' at Skegness on the east coast.

I taught children to swim for many years at all the camps, before applying to work at Borehamwood as the pool's senior swimming teacher. Looking back, these were the best times of my life— Butlins in the Summer, then travelling abroad for most of the Winter, chasing the sun.

I was invited by a friend to visit his private members' club, where I was treated to a most enjoyable day. It got me thinking about the opportunities for improvements at the swimming complex and I had a meeting with the club manager who seemed very interested in me working for him. I decided to take the job and set about a comprehensive reorganisation of every aspect connected with the pool and what if offered. The management were delighted.

From the pool, I moved on to the tennis section, followed by many other areas that needed change or improvement. I'm now in my twentieth year there. My home is in Hertfordshire where I live with my partner of many years, Christine. We are both very happy together.

If I had stayed in Enfield and not travelled to Australia, I would not have seen such wonderful places or met many truly remarkable people. *The day I became a 'Ten Pound Pom' changed my life forever.*

The Ten Pound Poms

Where did those fifty-four years go to?

John   *Jeff*   *Garry*

The author would like to dedicate some of his favourite poems to four special people who have sadly passed away.

For Doris Duthie, without whose sponsorship we would never have gone to Australia, and her son Gavin who passed away in 2017.

Do Not Stand At My Grave And Weep

Do not stand at my grave and weep; I am not there. I do not sleep.
I am a thousand winds that blow.
I am the diamond glints on snow.
I am the sunlight on ripened grain. I am the gentle autumn rain.
When you awake in the morning's hush
I am the swift uplifting rush
Of quiet birds in circled flight.
I am the soft stars that shine at night. Do not stand at my grave and cry;
I am not there. I did not die.

Anon.

For Hilda Robinson

Remember

Remember me when I am gone away, gone far away into the silent land;
When you can no more hold me by the hand, nor I half turn to go yet turning stay.
Remember me when no more day by day you tell me of our future that you planned:
Only remember me; you understand it will be late to counsel then or pray.
Yet if you should forget me for a while and afterwards remember, do not grieve:
For if the darkness and corruption leave a vestige of the thoughts that once I had,
Better by far you should forget and smile than you should remember and be sad.

Christina Rossetti (1830–1894)

167

For Moss Hollis

Footprints

One night a man dreamed he was walking along a beach with the Lord. Across the sky flashed scenes from his life in which there were two sets of footprints in the sand; one belonging to him, and the other to the Lord. But he saw that at the saddest points in his life, there was only one set of footprints. "Lord! You said that once I decided to follow you, you'd never leave me. So why, during my most troublesome times, is there only one set of footprints?"

The Lord replied, "My son, my precious child, I love you and would never leave you. During your times of trial and suffering, when you see only one set of footprints, it was then that I carried you."

Anon.

For Tony Robinson

A Smile

A smile costs nothing but gives much. It enriches those who receive without making poorer those who give. It takes but a moment, but the memory of it sometimes lasts forever.

None is so rich or mighty that he can get along without it, but none is so poor but that he can be made rich by it. A smile creates happiness in the home, fosters good will in business, and is the countersign of friendship.

It brings rest to the weary, cheer to the discouraged, sunshine to the sad, and it is nature's best antidote for trouble. Yet it cannot be bought, begged, borrowed or stolen, for it is something that is of no value to anyone until it is given away.

Some people are too tired to give you a smile, give them one of yours, as none needs a smile so much as he who has no more to give.

Anon.

www.ingramcontent.com/pod-product-compliance
Ingram Content Group UK Ltd.
Pitfield, Milton Keynes, MK11 3LW, UK
UKHW021102060425
457073UK00004B/198